MATTHEW FEARN

CGP
– books like no others!

CGP

It's another great book from CGP...

GCSE Additional Science is all about **understanding how science works**.
And not only that — understanding it well enough to be able to **question**
what you hear on TV and read in the papers.

But don't panic. This book includes all the **science facts** you need to learn,
and shows you how they work in the real world. It even includes
a **free** Online Edition you can read on your computer or tablet.

How to get your free Online Edition

Just go to **cgpbooks.co.uk/extras** and enter this code...

0621 0872 2824 1610

By the way, this code only works for one person. If somebody else has used
this book before you, they might have already claimed the Online Edition.

CGP — still the best! ☺

Our sole aim here at CGP is to produce the highest
quality books — carefully written, immaculately presented
and dangerously close to being funny.

Then we work our socks off to get them
out to you — at the cheapest possible prices.

Contents

HOW SCIENCE WORKS

The Scientific Process 1
Your Data's Got to Be Good 2
Benefits, Risks and Decision Making 3
Science Has Limits 4
Planning Experiments 5
Collecting, Processing and Presenting Data 6
Drawing Conclusions and Evaluating 8
The Controlled Assessment 9

B2 TOPIC 1 — GENES AND ENZYMES

Cells 10
Microscopes and DNA 11
More on DNA 12
Genes and Proteins 13
Enzymes 14
Enzyme Activity 15
More on Enzyme Activity 16
Genetic Engineering 17
Mitosis 18
Meiosis 19
Cloning Mammals 20
Stem Cells 21
Revision Summary for B2 Topic 1 22

B2 TOPIC 2 — LIFE PROCESSES

Respiration 23
Respiration and Exercise 24
Photosynthesis 25
The Rate of Photosynthesis 26
Osmosis 27
Water Uptake and Loss in Plants 28
Distribution — Pooters and Pitfall Traps 29
Distribution — Nets and Quadrats 30
More on Distribution 31
Revision Summary for B2 Topic 2 32

B2 TOPIC 3 — ORGAN SYSTEMS

Evidence for Evolution 33
Growth and Development 34
Cell Organisation and the Circulatory System 35
The Circulatory System — The Blood 36
The Circulatory System — Blood Vessels 37
Peristalsis and Digestive Enzymes 38
The Digestive System 39
Investigating Digestive Enzymes 40
Functional Foods 41
Revision Summary for B2 Topic 3 42

C2A TOPIC 1 — ATOMIC STRUCTURE AND THE PERIODIC TABLE

Atoms 43
Electron Shells 44
Elements and Numbers 45
A Brief History of the Periodic Table 46
The Periodic Table 47
Balancing Equations 48

C2A TOPIC 2 — IONIC COMPOUNDS AND ANALYSIS

Ionic Bonding 49
Ionic Compounds 50
Naming Compounds and Finding Formulas 51
Preparing Insoluble Salts 52
Barium Meals and Flame Tests 53
Testing for Negative Ions and Spectroscopy 54

C2A TOPIC 3 — COVALENT COMPOUNDS AND SEPARATION TECHNIQUES

Covalent Bonding 55
Covalent Substances — Two Kinds 56
Classifying Elements and Compounds 57
Separation Techniques 58
Chromatography 59
Revision Summary for C2a Topics 1, 2 & 3 60

C2B TOPIC 4 — GROUPS IN THE PERIODIC TABLE

Properties of Metals 61
Group 1 — The Alkali Metals 62
Group 7 — The Halogens 63
Group 0 — The Noble Gases 64

C2B TOPIC 5 — CHEMICAL REACTIONS

Energy Transfer in Reactions 65
Energy Changes and Measuring Temperature 66
Rates of Reaction 67
Rates of Reaction Experiments 68
Catalysts 70

C2B TOPIC 6 — QUANTITATIVE CHEMISTRY

Relative Formula Mass 71
Percentage Composition By Mass 72
Empirical Formulas 73
Percentage Yield 74
Revision Summary for C2b Topics 4, 5 & 6 75

P2A TOPIC 1 — STATIC AND CURRENT ELECTRICITY

Static Electricity 76
Uses and Dangers of Static Electricity 78
Charge and Current 79

P2A TOPIC 2 — CONTROLLING AND USING ELECTRIC CURRENT

Electric Current and Potential Difference 80
Resistance and $V = I \times R$ 81
Electrical Devices and Resistance 82
Electrical Power and Energy 83

P2A TOPIC 3 — MOTION AND FORCES

Velocity and Acceleration 84
D-T and V-T Graphs 85
Forces 86
Weight and Terminal Velocity 87
Forces and Motion 88
Force and Acceleration 89
Revision Summary for P2a Topics 1, 2 & 3 90

P2B TOPIC 4 — MOMENTUM, ENERGY, WORK AND POWER

Stopping Distances 91
Car Safety 92
Work and Power 93
Kinetic and Potential Energy 94
Conservation of Energy 95

P2B TOPIC 5 — NUCLEAR FISSION AND NUCLEAR FUSION

Radioactivity 96
Nuclear Fission and Fusion 98
Nuclear Power Stations 99

P2B TOPIC 6 — USING RADIOACTIVE MATERIALS

Background Radiation and Half-life 100
Calculating Half-life 101
Uses of Radioactivity 102
Dangers of Radioactivity 103
Nuclear Power 104
Revision Summary for P2b Topics 4, 5 & 6 105

Index 106
Answers 108

Published by CGP

From original material by Richard Parsons.

Editors:
Luke Antieul, Helena Hayes, Felicity Inkpen, Rosie McCurrie, Jane Sawers, Camilla Simson, Karen Wells, Sarah Williams, Dawn Wright.

Contributor:
Paddy Gannon.

ISBN: 978 1 84762 765 0

With thanks to Mark A Edwards, Mary Falkner, David Hickinson, Julie Jackson, Jamie Sinclair and Jane Towle for the proofreading.

Page 102 contains public sector information published by the Health and Safety Executive and licensed under the Open Government Licence v1.0.

Printed by Elanders Ltd, Newcastle upon Tyne.
Clipart from Corel®

The Scientific Process

For your <u>exams</u> and your <u>controlled assessment</u> you need to know about how the <u>world of science</u> works.

Science is All About *Testing a Hypothesis*

'Controlled assessment' is the scary name for the piece of coursework you have to do. See page 9 for more.

Scientists make an observation

1) Scientists <u>observe</u> (look at) something they don't understand — e.g. an illness that a person has.
2) Then they come up with a possible <u>explanation</u> for what they've observed.
3) This explanation is called a <u>HYPOTHESIS</u>.

Hundreds of years ago, we thought demons caused illness.

They test their hypothesis

1) Next, they <u>test</u> whether the hypothesis might be <u>right or not</u>.
2) They begin by making a <u>prediction</u> — a statement based on the hypothesis that can be <u>tested</u> by carrying out <u>experiments</u>.
3) Then they <u>collect evidence</u> (<u>data</u> from <u>experiments</u>) to test their prediction.
4) If their prediction is <u>right</u>, this shows that their <u>hypothesis might be right too</u>.

Then we thought it was caused by 'bad blood' (and treated it with leeches).

Other scientists test the hypothesis too

1) Other scientists carry out <u>more experiments</u> to test the hypothesis.
2) They'll also <u>check the results</u> of the original experiments by trying to <u>reproduce</u> them.
3) Sometimes the scientists will find <u>more evidence</u> that the <u>hypothesis is RIGHT</u>.
4) Sometimes they'll find <u>evidence</u> that shows the <u>hypothesis is WRONG</u>.

Now we know most illnesses are due to microorganisms.

The hypothesis is accepted or changed

1) If all the experiments back up the hypothesis, scientists start to have a lot of <u>trust</u> in it.
2) A hypothesis that's been <u>accepted</u> by most scientists in the world is called a <u>THEORY</u>.
3) But, if someone does an experiment and the results <u>don't</u> fit with the hypothesis then scientists must:
   a) <u>change</u> the hypothesis, OR
   b) come up with a completely <u>new</u> hypothesis.

You expect me to believe that — then show me the evidence...

If scientists think something is true, they need to find evidence to convince others. This is all part of <u>testing a hypothesis</u>. The hypothesis might survive these tests, but it might not. It's how science moves on.

Your Data's Got to Be Good

Evidence is the key to science — but not all evidence is equally good.

Lab Experiments and Studies Are Better Than Rumour

1) <u>Laboratory experiments</u> are <u>great</u>. A lab is the easiest place to <u>control the variables</u> in your experiment. This makes it easier to carry out a <u>FAIR TEST</u>.

2) For things that you <u>can't study in a lab</u> (e.g. climate) you carry out <u>scientific studies</u>. In studies, you control as many of the variables as possible.

3) Old wives' tales and rumours are <u>NOT scientific</u>. Without any evidence, they're just <u>opinions</u>.

See page 5 for more about fair tests and variables.

The Bigger the Sample Size the Better

1) Data based on <u>small samples</u> isn't as good as data based on large samples.

2) A sample should be as <u>similar</u> to the <u>whole population</u> as possible — i.e. it should share lots of characteristics with the population.

3) A small sample <u>can't do that</u> as well as a large sample.

Evidence Needs to be Reliable (Reproducible)

Evidence is only reliable if <u>other people can repeat it</u>. If they can't, then you can't believe it.

> RELIABLE means that the data can be <u>reproduced by others</u>.

<u>EXAMPLE</u>: In 1998, a scientist claimed that he'd found a link between the <u>MMR</u> (measles, mumps and rubella) <u>vaccine</u> and <u>autism</u>. Other scientists <u>couldn't</u> get the <u>same results</u> though — they <u>weren't reliable</u>.

Evidence Also Needs to Be Valid

> VALID means that the data is <u>reliable</u> AND <u>answers the original question</u>.

EXAMPLE: DO POWER LINES CAUSE CANCER?

- Some studies have found that in areas where there were <u>power lines</u>, <u>more children</u> had <u>cancer</u>.
- This evidence is <u>NOT enough</u> to say that the power lines <u>CAUSE</u> cancer. Other explanations might be possible, e.g. power lines are often near <u>busy roads</u>, so the areas tested could have <u>higher levels</u> of pollution from traffic. Pollution from traffic might be what's causing the cancer.
- As these studies <u>don't</u> show a <u>definite link</u> between power lines and cancer, they <u>don't answer the original question</u>.

Does the data really say that?...

If it's so hard to be <u>definite</u> about anything, how does anybody <u>ever</u> get convinced about anything? Well, what usually happens is that you get a <u>load</u> of evidence that all points the same way. Lots of evidence from <u>different experiments</u> tends to be more convincing than one little bit.

Benefits, Risks and Decision Making

Science is all about the <u>balance</u> between benefit and risk — a bit like life really...

Developments in Science Usually Have Benefits and Drawbacks...

Scientists have created loads of <u>new technologies</u> that could <u>improve</u> our lives.
For example, generating electricity using <u>nuclear power</u> has lots of <u>benefits</u>:

> 1) The <u>national population</u> benefits by getting <u>electricity</u>.
> 2) <u>Construction companies</u> benefit from years of work in building the power station.
> 3) <u>Local people</u> benefit from new jobs.

But it's not all good news.
One of the <u>drawbacks</u> is: ⟹ Nuclear power stations are <u>very expensive</u>.

...and They're Never Risk Free

1) Most technologies have some <u>risks</u>.
   For example, for a <u>new nuclear power station</u>:

   • Local people might be <u>exposed to high radiation levels</u>, which could affect their health.
   • There could be an <u>accident</u>, which would affect large areas.

2) Whether or not to build a new nuclear power station is a <u>big decision</u>.
3) To make a decision like this, people have to <u>weigh up</u> the benefits, drawbacks and risks.

Loads of Other Factors Can Influence Decisions Too

Here are some other factors that can influence decisions about science:

Economic (money) issues:
Governments <u>can't</u> always <u>afford</u> to do things scientists recommend, e.g. spend money on green energy sources.

Social (people) issues:
Decisions based on scientific evidence affect <u>people</u> — e.g. should alcohol be banned to prevent health problems?

Ethical (rights and wrongs) issues:
There are a lot of things science has made possible, but <u>should we do them</u>? E.g. develop better nuclear weapons.

Environmental issues:
<u>Genetically modified crops</u> may help us <u>produce more food</u> — but some people think they could cause <u>environmental problems</u>.

Not revising — a definite drawback in the exam...

Developments in science involve a lot of <u>weighing up</u> — new technologies have risks, but the benefits are often huge. Then there are the economic, social, environmental and ethical issues to think about...

Science Has Limits

Science can give us amazing things — cures for diseases, space travel, heated toilet seats...
But science has its limitations — there are questions that it just can't answer.

Some Questions Are Unanswered by Science — So Far

1) There are some things we don't understand:

   > EXAMPLES:
   >
   > - Today we don't know as much as we'd like about the impacts of global warming.
   >   How much will sea level rise? And how will weather patterns change?
   > - We also don't know anywhere near as much as we'd like about the Universe.
   >   Are there other life forms out there? And what is the Universe made of?

2) These are difficult questions — scientists don't agree on the answers.

3) This is because there isn't enough evidence.

4) Eventually, we probably will be able to answer these questions once and for all.

5) All we need is more evidence.

Other Questions Are Unanswerable by Science

1) The question of whether we should or shouldn't do something
   can't ever be answered by more experiments.

2) That's because there is no "right" or "wrong" answer.

3) Take space exploration. It's possible to do it — but does that mean we should?

4) Different people have different opinions.

> For example...
> Some people say it's a good idea... it increases our knowledge about the
> Universe, we develop new technologies that can be useful on Earth too,
> it inspires young people to take an interest in science, etc.
>
> Other people say it's a bad idea... the vast sums of money it costs should
> be spent on more urgent problems, like providing clean drinking water and
> curing diseases in poor countries. Others say that we should concentrate
> research efforts on understanding our own planet better first.

5) The best we can do is make a decision that most people are more or less happy to live by.

Chips or rice? — totally unanswerable by science...

Right — get this straight in your head — science can't tell you whether you should or shouldn't do something.
That kind of thing is up to you and society to decide. There are tons of questions that science might be able
to answer in the future — like how much sea level might rise due to global warming, what the Universe is
made of and whatever happened to those pink stripy socks with Santa on that I used to have.

Planning Experiments

The next few pages show how <u>experiments</u> should be carried out — by both <u>professional scientists</u> and <u>you</u>.

An Experiment Must be a Fair Test

1) You need to make sure that the <u>evidence</u> you collect is <u>valid</u> and <u>reliable</u> (see page 2).
   This means that your experiment must be a <u>fair test</u>.

2) The only way to make it a fair test is to <u>change</u> only <u>one variable</u> (factor) in the experiment.

3) All the <u>other variables</u> should <u>be controlled</u> — they should <u>stay exactly the same</u>.
   For example, if you're looking at the effect of <u>temperature</u> on the rate of an enzyme-controlled reaction, you need to keep the <u>pH</u> the same each time.

The Equipment Used Has to be Right for the Job

1) When you're planning an experiment, you need to make sure you choose the <u>right equipment</u>.

2) For example, the measuring equipment you use has to be able to <u>accurately</u> measure the chemicals you're using. If you need to measure out 11 ml of a liquid, use a measuring cylinder that can measure to 1 ml, not 5 or 10 ml.

Accurate measurements are really close to the true value of what you're measuring.

An Experiment Must be Safe

1) There are lots of <u>hazards</u> (dangers) you could be faced with during an investigation, e.g. <u>radiation</u>, <u>electricity</u>, <u>gas</u>, <u>chemicals</u> and <u>fire</u>.

2) You should always make sure that you think of <u>all</u> the hazards there might be.

3) You should also come up with ways of <u>reducing the risks</u> from the hazards you've spotted.

4) You can do this in a <u>risk assessment</u>.
   For example, for an experiment involving a <u>Bunsen burner</u>:

<u>Hazard</u>: Bunsen burner is a fire risk.
<u>Ways risk can be reduced</u>:
- Keep chemicals that can catch fire away from the Bunsen.
- Never leave the Bunsen alone when lit.
- Always turn on the yellow safety flame when not in use.

Repeats affect Reliability, and Range of Measurements affects Validity

1) To make your data <u>more reliable</u>, <u>repeat</u> the measurements and take an <u>average</u> (see next page).

2) You also need to think about the <u>range of data</u> you collect (i.e. what your highest and lowest measurements will be). Make sure you take <u>enough measurements</u> throughout the range too.

3) If the range isn't big enough, or you don't take enough measurements, your data <u>won't</u> be <u>valid</u> for the <u>hypothesis</u> you're testing.

Take a look back at page 2 if you can't remember what reliability and validity are.

Reliable data — it won't ever forget your birthday...

All this stuff is really important — without <u>good quality</u> data an investigation will be totally <u>meaningless</u>. So give this page a read through a couple of times and your data will be the envy of <u>every scientist in the world</u>.

Collecting, Processing and Presenting Data

The fun doesn't stop once you've collected your data — it then needs to be **processed** and presented...

Data **Needs to be Organised**

1) Data that's been collected needs to be organised so it can be processed later on.
2) Tables are dead useful for organising data.
3) When you're drawing a table, make sure that each column has a heading and that you've included the units.

Check For Mistakes Made When Collecting Data

1) When you've collected all your results, have a look to see if there are any that don't seem to fit.
2) Most results vary a bit, but any that are totally different are called anomalous results.
3) If you ever get any anomalous results, you should try to work out what happened.
4) If you can work out what happened (e.g. you measured something wrong) you can ignore the result.

Data **Can be Processed** Using a Bit of Maths

1) Raw data just isn't that useful. To make it useful, you have to process it in some way.
2) One of the most simple calculations you can do is the mean (average):

To calculate the mean **ADD TOGETHER** all the data values. Then **DIVIDE** by the total number of values. You usually do this to get a single value from several repeats of your experiment.

Test tube	Result (ml)	Repeat 1 (ml)	Repeat 2 (ml)	Mean (ml)
A	28	37	32	(28 + 37 + 32) ÷ 3 = 32.3
B	47	51	60	(47 + 51 + 60) ÷ 3 = 52.7
C	68	72	70	(68 + 72 + 70) ÷ 3 = 70.0

If Your Data Comes in Categories, Present It in a Bar Chart

1) If one of the variables comes in clear categories (e.g. blood types) use a bar chart to display the data.
2) There are some golden rules you need to follow for drawing bar charts:

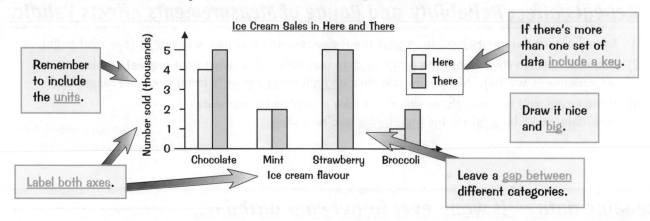

Remember to include the units.

If there's more than one set of data include a key.

Draw it nice and big.

Label both axes.

Leave a gap between different categories.

How Science Works

Collecting, Processing and Presenting Data

If Your Data Can Have Any Value, Plot a Line Graph

1) If both the variables can have any value within a range (e.g. length, volume, temperature) you should use a line graph to display the data.

2) Here are the rules for drawing line graphs:

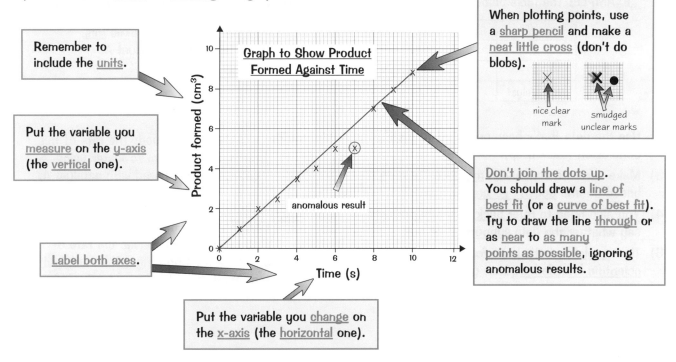

Remember to include the units.

Put the variable you measure on the y-axis (the vertical one).

Label both axes.

Put the variable you change on the x-axis (the horizontal one).

When plotting points, use a sharp pencil and make a neat little cross (don't do blobs).

nice clear mark

smudged unclear marks

Don't join the dots up. You should draw a line of best fit (or a curve of best fit). Try to draw the line through or as near to as many points as possible, ignoring anomalous results.

Graph to Show Product Formed Against Time

anomalous result

Line Graphs Can Show Relationships in Data

1) Line graphs are used to show the relationship between two variables (just like other graphs).

2) Data can show different types of correlation (relationship):

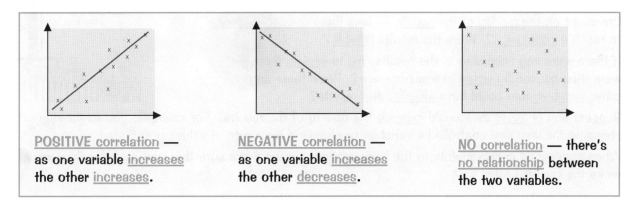

POSITIVE correlation — as one variable increases the other increases.

NEGATIVE correlation — as one variable increases the other decreases.

NO correlation — there's no relationship between the two variables.

3) Don't confuse correlation with cause.

4) A correlation just means that there's a relationship between two variables. It doesn't mean that the change in one variable is causing the change in the other (there might be other factors involved).

There's a positive correlation between age of man and length of nose hair...

Collect, process, present... data's like a difficult child — it needs a lot of attention. Go on, make it happy.

Drawing Conclusions and Evaluating

At the end of an experiment, the conclusion and evaluation are waiting. Don't worry, they won't bite.

You Can Only Conclude What the Data Shows and NO MORE

1) To come to a conclusion, look at your data and say what pattern you see.

EXAMPLE: The table below shows the rate of a reaction in the presence of two different catalysts.

Catalyst	Rate of reaction (cm³/s)
A	13.5
B	19.5
No catalyst	5.5

CONCLUSION: Catalyst B makes this reaction go faster than catalyst A.

2) Use the data that's been collected to justify the conclusion (back it up).

3) Make sure the conclusion matches the data it's based on and doesn't go any further.

EXAMPLE continued: The rate of this reaction was 6 cm³/s faster using catalyst B compared with catalyst A.

4) You also need to refer back to the hypothesis — say whether the data supports it or not.

5) Then explain what's been found using your own scientific knowledge (what you've learnt in class).

EXAMPLE continued: You can't conclude that catalyst B increases the rate of any other reaction more than catalyst A — the results might be completely different.

Evaluation — Describe How You Could Improve the Investigation

1) You should comment on the method — was the equipment suitable? Was it a fair test?

2) Comment on the quality of the results — was there enough evidence to reach a conclusion? Were the results reliable?

3) If there were any anomalies in the results, try to explain them — were they caused by errors in measurement? Were there any other variables that could have affected the results?

4) Suggest any changes that would improve the quality of the results. For example, you might suggest changing the way you controlled a variable, or changing the range of values you tested.

5) When suggesting improvements to the investigation, always make sure that you say why they would make the results better.

I'd value this E somewhere in the region of 250-300k

E

Evaluation — next time, I will make sure I don't burn the lab down...

I know it doesn't seem very nice, but writing about where you went wrong is an important skill. It shows you've got a really good understanding of what the investigation was about. It's difficult for me — I'm always right.

The Controlled Assessment

You'll probably carry out a few investigations as you go through the course. But at some point you'll have to do the one that counts... the controlled assessment. Here's a bit about it, but make sure you can recite all the stuff we've covered in this section first — it'll really help you out.

The Controlled Assessment is Split into Three Parts

Part A — Planning

For this part you'll be given some information about a topic. Then you'll have to develop a hypothesis and plan an experiment to test it. Write a method in a logical step-by-step order — you'll need to decide:

1) What variables you're going to control — and how you're going to control them.
2) What equipment to use — and say why you've chosen each bit of kit.
3) What risks are involved in the experiment — and say how you're going to reduce each of them.
4) The range of measurements you're going to take — and say why you've chosen that range.
5) How many times you'll repeat each measurement. You should do at least two repeats to make your data more reliable.

There's lots of help on all of these things on page 5.

Part B — Observations

For this part you'll be given a new hypothesis and an experiment plan.
You then follow the plan and carry out the experiment. You'll need to:

1) Take an appropriate number and range of measurements (see page 5).
2) Repeat your measurements to get more reliable data (if possible).
3) Record your data clearly in a nice, neat table (see page 6 for table tips).

Part C — Conclusions

This part involves processing data, presenting data, drawing conclusions and evaluating.
You'll have to do these things for your data (primary data) and also for data collected by other people (secondary data). You'll be given the secondary data when you need it. You'll need to:

1) Process all the data (both primary and secondary), e.g. calculate the mean (see page 6).
2) Present all the data using the right type of graph for each (see pages 6-7 for help with this).
3) Spot any anomalous results. If there aren't any anomalous results, then you need to say so.
4) Write a conclusion for both sets of data (see previous page for what to say).
5) Write an evaluation (see previous page for what to include).

Keep your assessment under control — read this page...

Pretty straightforward, eh? As long as you've learnt everything on the previous few pages, you should be fine. Make sure you know each section like the back of your hand before you come to do the assessment itself.

Cells

All living things are made of cells. They're the building blocks of every organism on the planet...

Plant and Animal Cells have Similarities and Differences

Animal Cell

4 things they both have in common:

1) NUCLEUS — contains DNA that controls what the cell does.

2) CYTOPLASM — gel-like substance where most of the chemical reactions happen.

3) CELL MEMBRANE — holds the cell together and controls what goes in and out.

4) MITOCHONDRIA — these are where most of the reactions for respiration take place. (Respiration releases energy that the cell needs to work.)

Plant Cell

3 extras that only the plant cell has:

1) CELL WALL — made of cellulose, gives support for the cell.

2) LARGE VACUOLE — contains cell sap (a sugar and salt solution).

3) CHLOROPLASTS — where photosynthesis occurs. (Photosynthesis is how plants make food.)

Bacterial Cells Have No Nucleus

Bacterial cells are a lot smaller than plant or animal cells. They have these features:

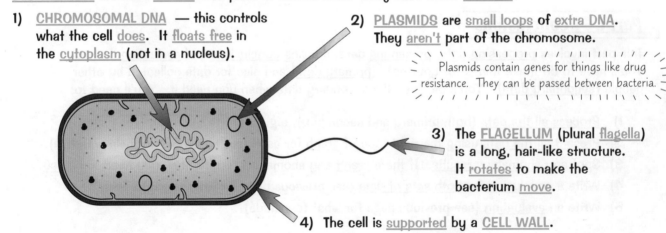

1) CHROMOSOMAL DNA — this controls what the cell does. It floats free in the cytoplasm (not in a nucleus).

2) PLASMIDS are small loops of extra DNA. They aren't part of the chromosome.

Plasmids contain genes for things like drug resistance. They can be passed between bacteria.

3) The FLAGELLUM (plural flagella) is a long, hair-like structure. It rotates to make the bacterium move.

4) The cell is supported by a CELL WALL.

There's quite a bit to learn in biology — but that's life, I guess...

On this page are typical cells with all the typical bits you need to know. Why not practise labelling them and making sure you know the key features of each cell type. Ahhhh the joys of revision. Go on, get stuck in...

Microscopes and DNA

Microscopes make little things look <u>bigger</u>. This allows scientists to study cells in <u>more detail</u>...

Cells are Studied Using Microscopes

1) <u>Microscopes</u> let us see things that we <u>can't see</u> with the <u>naked eye</u>.

2) You can use a <u>light microscope</u> to see <u>small things</u> in <u>more detail</u>, e.g. the nucleus of a cell.

3) <u>Electron microscopes</u> are <u>more powerful</u> than light microscopes. They let you see <u>even smaller things</u> in <u>even more detail</u>.

4) You need to be able to calculate <u>magnification</u>. Magnification is how much <u>bigger</u> the <u>image</u> is than the <u>specimen</u> (the sample you're looking at).

5) It's <u>calculated</u> using this formula:

$$\text{magnification} = \frac{\text{length of image}}{\text{length of specimen}}$$

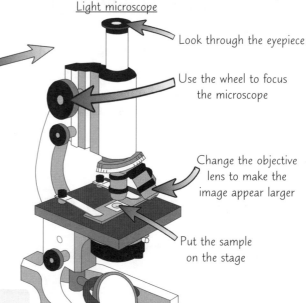

Light microscope

Look through the eyepiece

Use the wheel to focus the microscope

Change the objective lens to make the image appear larger

Put the sample on the stage

Adjust the mirror to make sure there's plenty of light

EXAMPLE

Your specimen is <u>0.05 mm</u> wide.
Your magnified image is <u>5 mm</u> wide.
Put the values into the formula:

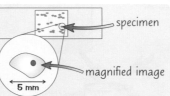

specimen

magnified image

5 mm

$$\text{magnification} = \frac{\text{length of image}}{\text{length of specimen}} \longrightarrow \frac{5}{0.05} = 100 \text{ so it's} \times 100 \text{ magnification.}$$

DNA — a Double Helix of Paired Bases

1) A DNA molecule has <u>two strands</u> coiled together in the shape of a <u>double helix</u> (two spirals).

2) The two strands are <u>held together</u> by chemicals called <u>bases</u>.

3) There are <u>four</u> different bases (shown in the diagram as different colours) — <u>adenine</u> (A), <u>cytosine</u> (C), <u>guanine</u> (G) and <u>thymine</u> (T).

4) The bases are <u>paired</u>.

5) They always pair up in the same way — it's always A-T and C-G. This is called <u>base-pairing</u>.

6) The <u>base pairs</u> are joined together by <u>weak hydrogen bonds</u>.

7) A <u>gene</u> is a <u>section</u> of DNA.

8) The <u>sequence of bases</u> in a gene <u>code</u> for a <u>specific protein</u> — see page 13 for more.

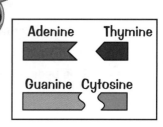

Adenine   Thymine

Guanine Cytosine

The DNA double helix — a colourful spiral staircase...

The <u>DNA double helix</u> is one of the most famous images in biology. Remember — it's A with T, and C with G. Don't forget <u>magnification</u> calculations either — <u>learn the formula</u> and <u>plug in the numbers</u>. It's jolly good fun.

More on DNA

Scientists have done loads of studies on the structure of DNA. Now get ready to do your own experiment...

Watson, Crick, Franklin and Wilkins Discovered The Structure of DNA

1) Rosalind Franklin and Maurice Wilkins worked out that DNA had a helical (spiral) structure.
2) They found this out by firing beams of x-rays onto a crystal of DNA and looking at the patterns this made.
3) James Watson and Francis Crick used these findings to make a model of DNA.
4) From the studies of other scientists, they knew that the amount of A + G matched the amount of T + C.
5) Watson and Crick used all this information to make a model of DNA where all the pieces fitted together.

A, G, T and C are DNA bases (see p.11).

You Can Do a Practical To Extract DNA From Cells

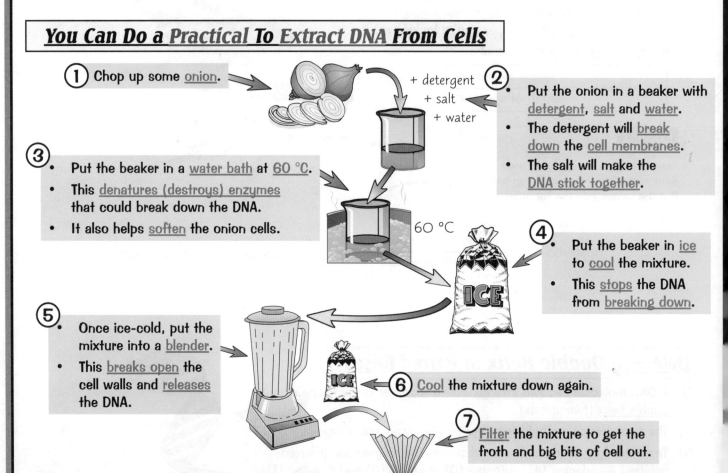

① Chop up some onion.

②
- Put the onion in a beaker with detergent, salt and water.
- The detergent will break down the cell membranes.
- The salt will make the DNA stick together.

+ detergent
+ salt
+ water

③
- Put the beaker in a water bath at 60 °C.
- This denatures (destroys) enzymes that could break down the DNA.
- It also helps soften the onion cells.

60 °C

④
- Put the beaker in ice to cool the mixture.
- This stops the DNA from breaking down.

⑤
- Once ice-cold, put the mixture into a blender.
- This breaks open the cell walls and releases the DNA.

⑥ Cool the mixture down again.

⑦ Filter the mixture to get the froth and big bits of cell out.

⑧
- Gently add some ice-cold alcohol.
- The DNA will start to come out of solution.
- This is because it's not soluble in cold alcohol.

+ alcohol

⑨ The DNA will appear as a stringy white substance. You can fish it out with a glass rod.

DNA extraction — makes your eyes water...

Hope you enjoyed extracting all that DNA. You're too late to get a Nobel prize for your efforts though — Crick, Watson and Wilkins beat you to it in 1962. (Unfortunately Franklin had died by then so couldn't be nominated.)

Genes and Proteins

Your DNA is just a long list of <u>instructions</u>. It tells your cells how to make <u>all the proteins</u> in your body.

A Gene Codes for a Specific Protein

1) A <u>gene</u> is a <u>section</u> of DNA.
2) This section of DNA contains the <u>instructions</u> to make a <u>specific protein</u>.
3) Cells make <u>proteins</u> by putting <u>amino acids</u> together in a particular order.
4) Only <u>20</u> different amino acids are used to make up <u>thousands</u> of different <u>proteins</u>.
5) The <u>order of the bases</u> in a gene tells cells the <u>order</u> of the amino acids.

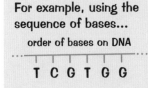

For example, using the sequence of bases...

order of bases on DNA

T C G T G G

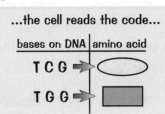

...the cell reads the code...

bases on DNA	amino acid
T C G →	⬭
T G G →	▬

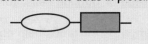

... to put these amino acids together.

order of amino acids in protein

A Protein's Shape is Essential for it's Job

1) Each type of <u>protein</u> gets made with its own specific <u>number</u> and <u>order</u> of <u>amino acids</u>.
2) This is what makes a protein <u>fold up into the right shape</u> to do its specific <u>job</u>, e.g. as a particular <u>enzyme</u> (see the next page).
3) If it's <u>not</u> the <u>right shape</u>, it might <u>not</u> be able to do it's <u>job</u> properly.

Mutations can be Harmful, Beneficial or Neutral

1) A <u>mutation</u> is a <u>change</u> to an organism's <u>DNA base sequence</u>.
2) A mutation could change the order of <u>amino acids</u> in a protein.
3) This could change the <u>shape</u> of the protein...and so it could change its <u>function</u>.
4) In turn, this could change the <u>characteristics</u> (features) of an organism.
5) Mutations can be <u>harmful</u> (bad), <u>beneficial</u> (good), or <u>neutral</u> (not bad or good):

HARMFUL   A mutation could cause a <u>genetic disorder</u> (a disease that you get from your parents). E.g. <u>cystic fibrosis</u> (a disease that affects the cell membranes).

BENEFICIAL   A mutation could produce a <u>new characteristic</u> that is <u>beneficial</u> (helpful) to an organism. E.g. a mutation in genes on bacterial plasmids can make them <u>resistant</u> to <u>antibiotics</u>.

NEUTRAL   Some mutations <u>aren't harmful or beneficial</u>. E.g. they don't change a protein's function.

Resistant means they're not killed.

4 bases, 20 amino acids, 1000s of proteins...

The <u>order of bases</u> says what amino acid is added and the <u>order of amino acids</u> determines the type of protein.

Enzymes

Chemical reactions are what make you work. And enzymes are what make them work.

Enzymes Are Catalysts Made by Living Things

1) Living things have tons of chemical reactions going on inside them all the time.

2) Living things produce enzymes. Enzymes act as biological catalysts.

3) Enzymes speed up the useful chemical reactions in the body.

> A CATALYST is a substance which INCREASES the speed of a reaction, without being CHANGED or USED UP in the reaction.

4) Enzymes are all proteins.

5) Enzymes all work in the same way to catalyse (speed up) various reactions.

6) They can work inside or outside cells, for example:

- DNA replication — enzymes help copy a cell's DNA before it divides.
- Protein synthesis (making proteins) — enzymes hold amino acids in place and form bonds between them.
- Digestion — enzymes are released into the gut to digest food.

Enzymes Have Special Shapes

1) Chemical reactions usually mean things get split apart or joined together.

2) The substrate is the molecule changed in the reaction.

3) Every enzyme has an active site. This is the part where it joins on to its substrate.

4) Enzymes are really picky — they usually only work with one substrate. The posh way of saying this is that enzymes are highly specific for their substrate.

5) The substrate has to fit into the active site for the enzyme to work.

6) This is called the 'lock and key' mechanism. This is because the substrate fits into the enzyme just like a key fits into a lock.

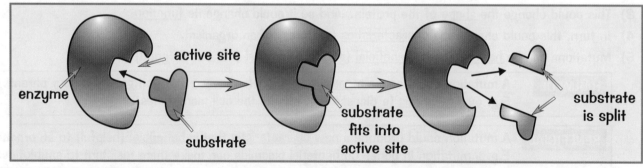

If the substrate's shape doesn't match the active site's shape, then the reaction won't happen.

If the lock & key mechanism fails, you get in through a window...

Just like you've got to have the correct key for a lock, you've got to have the right substrate for an enzyme.

Enzyme Activity

Now you know a bit about <u>enzymes</u>, you can do an <u>investigation</u> to see how they really <u>work</u>...

Measuring Enzyme Activity — Method

1) You can <u>measure</u> the <u>rate of a reaction</u> that is catalysed by an enzyme. For example:

The rate of a reaction means how quickly it happens.

- Use <u>amylase</u> as the <u>enzyme</u>.
- Use <u>starch</u> as the <u>substrate</u>.

2) <u>Amylase</u> breaks down <u>starch</u>. This means you can <u>time</u> how long it takes for the <u>starch</u> to <u>disappear</u>.

3) Here's what you do...

1) Take a <u>drop</u> of the <u>amylase and starch</u> mixture every minute.

2) Put it onto a drop of <u>iodine solution</u> on a spotting tile.

3) Record any <u>change in colour</u>. The iodine solution will turn <u>blue-black</u> if <u>starch</u> is there.

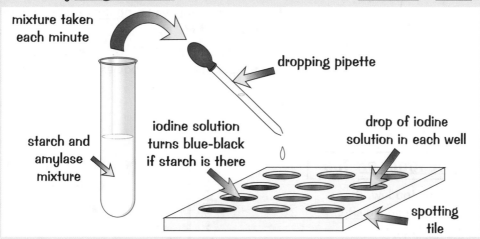

mixture taken each minute

dropping pipette

starch and amylase mixture

iodine solution turns blue-black if starch is there

drop of iodine solution in each well

spotting tile

4) Note the <u>time</u> when the iodine solution <u>no longer</u> turns blue-black.

5) This means all the starch has been <u>broken down</u> by the amylase.

Measuring Enzyme Activity — Variables

In the amylase/starch experiment above, you need to choose which <u>variable</u> to <u>change</u>. For example, to look at the effect of:

① <u>Temperature</u>	Put the test tubes into <u>water baths</u> at a range of temperatures.
② <u>pH</u>	Use a range of different <u>pH buffers</u>.
③ <u>Substrate Concentration</u>	Vary the <u>concentrations</u> of the <u>starch solutions</u> that you start with.

Remember to keep all the variables you're not investigating the same. E.g. use the same amylase concentration each time.

My reaction to enzymes — I'm amylased...

So that's how you set up the <u>method</u> for measuring enzyme activity. Then, you can use the <u>time</u> when the iodine solution no longer turns blue-black to <u>compare reaction rates</u> under <u>different conditions</u>. Fun times... read on...

More on Enzyme Activity

I bet you're dying to know the results of measuring enzyme activity under different conditions. No... oh well...

Measuring Enzyme Activity — Results

Enzymes Like it Warm but Not Too Hot

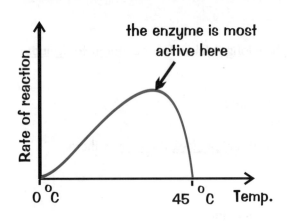

the enzyme is most active here

1) A higher temperature increases the rate of a reaction at first.

2) If it gets too hot though, some of the bonds holding the enzyme together break.

3) This makes the enzyme lose its shape. Its active site doesn't fit the shape of the substrate any more.

4) The enzyme is denatured. This means it's destroyed and won't go back to its normal shape.

5) All enzymes have an optimum temperature that they work best at.

6) It's usually about 37 °C. This is the same temperature as our bodies. Lucky for us.

Enzymes Like it the Right pH Too

1) If the pH is too high or too low, it changes the shape of the active site.

2) This denatures the enzyme.

3) An enzyme's optimum pH is often neutral pH 7, but not always. For example, an enzyme called pepsin works best in the acidic conditions of the stomach.

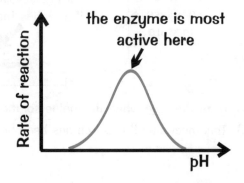

the enzyme is most active here

Substrate Concentration Affects the Rate of Reaction Up to a Point

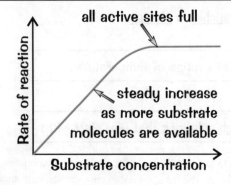

all active sites full

steady increase as more substrate molecules are available

1) The higher the substrate concentration, the faster the reaction.

2) This is because there are more substrate molecules for the enzyme to react with.

3) But after a point, there are so many substrate molecules that all the active sites are full.

4) After this point, adding more substrate makes no difference to the rate of reaction.

If only enzymes could speed up revision...

Changing the shape of a protein totally changes it. Egg white contains lots of protein — think what happens when you boil an egg and denature (destroy) the protein. It goes from clear and runny to white and solid.

Genetic Engineering

Scientists can now <u>change</u> an organism's <u>genes</u>. This is pretty exciting stuff, but there may be <u>dangers</u> too...

Genetic Engineering <u>Uses</u> Enzymes to Cut and Paste Genes

1) A useful gene is "<u>cut</u>" out from one organism's chromosome using <u>enzymes</u>.

2) <u>Enzymes</u> are then used to <u>cut</u> another organism's chromosome and then to <u>insert</u> the useful gene.

3) Moving about genes like this produces organisms called <u>genetically modified</u> (<u>GM</u>) organisms.
E.g. <u>human genes</u> can be used to make <u>GM bacteria</u>:

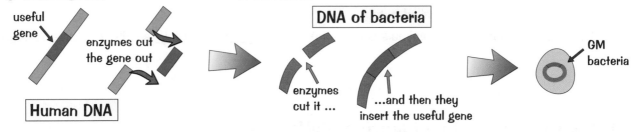

Genetic Engineering <u>has Some</u> Advantages:

① It can reduce vitamin A deficiency

1) Vitamin A <u>deficiency</u> means you don't get <u>enough</u> vitamin A. It can make you go <u>blind</u>.

2) Beta-carotene is used by our bodies to make <u>vitamin A</u>.

3) <u>Golden Rice</u> is a type of GM rice. It contains <u>genes</u> from other organisms.
These genes allow Golden Rice to produce <u>beta-carotene</u>.

4) Growing Golden Rice could mean <u>fewer people</u> will suffer from <u>vitamin A deficiency</u>.

② It can be used to make human insulin

1) The <u>human insulin gene</u> can be put into <u>bacteria</u> to make <u>human insulin</u>.

2) <u>Lots</u> of human insulin can be made <u>quickly</u> and <u>cheaply</u> to <u>treat diabetes</u>.

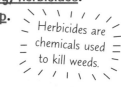
Diabetes is a condition where a person's blood sugar level gets too high. Insulin lowers blood sugar level.

③ It can increase crop yield (amount of food)

1) <u>GM crops</u> have had their genes changed, e.g. to make them <u>resistant to (not killed by) herbicides</u>.

2) Fields can be <u>sprayed</u> with a herbicide. This will kill <u>all the plants</u> except the <u>GM crop</u>.

3) This can <u>increase the yield</u> of the crop, making <u>more food</u>.

Herbicides are chemicals used to kill weeds.

But Some People <u>have</u> Concerns...

There's a risk that genetic engineering could cause <u>problems</u>. Some people have worries about <u>GM crops</u>, e.g:

1) Growing GM crops could affect the number of <u>flowers</u> and <u>insects</u> that live by <u>crops</u>.

2) Some people think GM crops are <u>not safe</u> to <u>eat</u>.

3) <u>GM genes</u> may get out into the <u>natural environment</u>. E.g. the <u>herbicide resistance</u> gene may be picked up by weeds. This could create a '<u>superweed</u>' — a weed that <u>can't be killed</u> by herbicides.

I say it's great.

GM crops — that's nothing... my American cousin had a GM car...

There are <u>good points</u> and <u>bad points</u> about genetic engineering... you need to learn <u>both sides</u> of the argument.

Mitosis

Your cells <u>divide</u> to <u>produce more cells.</u> This is so that your body can <u>grow</u> and <u>repair</u> damaged tissues...

Mitosis Makes New Cells for Growth and Repair

1) <u>Human body cells</u> are <u>diploid</u>. This means they have <u>two copies</u> of each <u>chromosome</u>.

2) One copy comes from the person's <u>mother</u>. The other copy comes from the <u>father</u>.

3) When a body cell <u>divides</u> it needs to make <u>two</u> cells <u>identical</u> to the <u>original</u> cell — with the <u>same number</u> of chromosomes.

4) This type of cell division is called <u>mitosis</u>.

5) It's used when humans (and animals and plants) want to <u>grow</u> or to <u>replace</u> cells that have been <u>damaged</u>.

> There are 23 pairs of chromosomes in a human cell.

Mitosis Produces Two Identical Cells

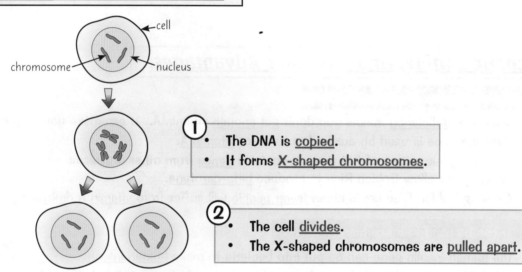

① • The DNA is <u>copied</u>.
• It forms <u>X-shaped chromosomes</u>.

② • The cell <u>divides</u>.
• The X-shaped chromosomes are <u>pulled apart</u>.

• You now have <u>two new diploid cells</u>.
• They contain exactly the <u>same DNA</u> — they're <u>genetically identical</u>.

Asexual Reproduction Also Uses Mitosis

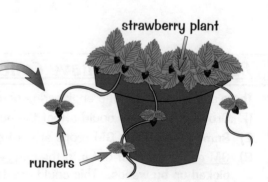

strawberry plant

1) Some organisms <u>reproduce</u> by mitosis. For example, <u>strawberry plants</u> form <u>runners</u> using mitosis. The runners become <u>new plants</u>.

2) This is an example of <u>asexual reproduction</u>.

3) The offspring (new strawberry plants) have exactly the <u>same genes</u> as the parent. This means there's <u>no genetic variation</u>.

runners

Now that I have your undivided attention...

Make sure that you learn <u>mitosis</u> really well, before moving onto the next page. Remember <u>mitosis</u> produces <u>two genetically identical, diploid cells</u> and it's used for <u>growth</u>, <u>repair</u> and in <u>asexual reproduction</u>.

Meiosis

You thought mitosis was exciting. Hah. This stuff <u>beats</u> it hands down. Seriously.

Gametes Have Half the Usual Number of Chromosomes

1) <u>Gametes</u> are 'sex cells'. They're called <u>ova</u> (single, ovum) in females. They're called <u>sperm</u> in males.

2) During <u>sexual reproduction</u>, two <u>gametes combine</u> to form a <u>new cell</u>.

3) <u>Gametes</u> are <u>haploid</u> — this means they only have <u>one copy</u> of each <u>chromosome</u>.

4) This is so that when <u>two gametes combine</u> at fertilisation, the resulting cell (called a <u>zygote</u>) has the <u>right number of chromosomes</u>.

5) Zygotes are <u>diploid</u> — they have <u>two copies</u> of each <u>chromosome</u>.

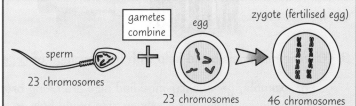

Human body cells have <u>46 chromosomes</u>. The gametes have <u>23 chromosomes each</u>. When an egg and sperm combine, you get <u>46 chromosomes</u> again. Clever.

Meiosis Produces Four Different Cells

1) Meiosis <u>only</u> happens in the <u>reproductive organs</u> (the ovaries and testes).

2) <u>Meiosis</u> is when a cell divides to produce <u>four haploid cells</u> whose <u>chromosomes are NOT identical</u>.

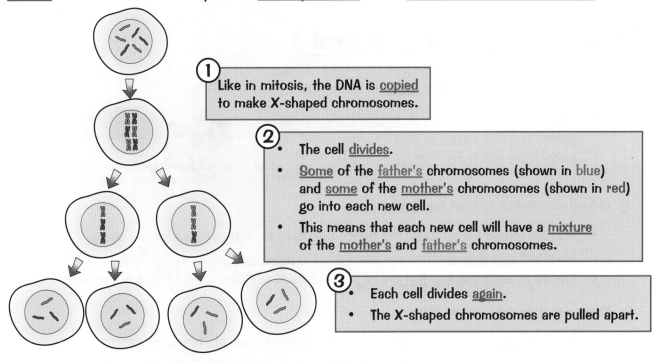

① Like in mitosis, the DNA is <u>copied</u> to make X-shaped chromosomes.

② • The cell <u>divides</u>.
   • <u>Some</u> of the <u>father's</u> chromosomes (shown in blue) and <u>some</u> of the <u>mother's</u> chromosomes (shown in red) go into each new cell.
   • This means that each new cell will have a <u>mixture</u> of the <u>mother's</u> and <u>father's</u> chromosomes.

③ • Each cell divides <u>again</u>.
   • The X-shaped chromosomes are pulled apart.

• You end up with <u>four haploid gametes</u>.
• Each gamete only has a <u>one copy</u> of each chromosome in it.
• Each gamete is <u>genetically different</u>.

You need to reproduce these facts in the exam...

So that's <u>meiosis</u>. You get <u>four genetically different haploid cells</u> and it only happens in the <u>reproductive organs</u>.

Cloning Mammals

Cloning means making identical copies of something. Try and clone the stuff on this page into your brain...

Cloning has Many Uses...

1) Cloning is a type of asexual reproduction (see page 18).

2) It produces cells that are genetically identical to an original cell.

3) Cloning mammals could help with the shortage of organs for transplants.

> For example, genetically-modified pigs are being bred that could provide suitable organs for humans. If this works, then cloning these pigs could help to meet the demand for organ transplants.

4) Studying animal clones could improve our understanding of things like ageing, age-related disorders and the development of embryos.

5) Cloning could be used to help preserve endangered species (save groups of animals that are at risk of being wiped out).

...But there are also Issues Involved

1) Cloning mammals leads to a "reduced gene pool" — this means there are fewer different alleles in a population.

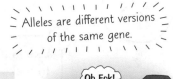
Alleles are different versions of the same gene.

Oh Eck!

> • If a population are all closely related (have similar genes) and a new disease appears, they could all be wiped out. This is because there may be no allele in the population giving resistance to the disease.

2) Cloned mammals might not live as long.

> • The first cloned animal (Dolly the sheep) only lived for half as long as many sheep.
> • Dolly had lung disease. This was more usual in older sheep.
> • But it's possible she was just unlucky — and that her illness wasn't linked to her being a clone.

3) There are other risks and problems to do with cloning:

> • The cloning process often fails. It took hundreds of attempts to clone Dolly.
> • Clones are often born with genetic defects (things wrong with their genes).
> • Cloned mammals' immune systems are sometimes unhealthy — so they suffer from more diseases.

Thank goodness they didn't do that with my little brother...

Cloning is exciting. Sci-Fi writers love it. But it's a tricky topic — it has many advantages, but it has risks too. Hmmm... a bit like swimming with sharks I guess — it has the advantage of being fun but the risk of being eaten.

Stem Cells

Cells divide to make you grow. They also <u>differentiate</u> (specialise) so that they can do different jobs.

Embryonic Stem Cells *Can Turn into Any Type of Cell*

1)   A fertilised egg can divide to produce a bundle of cells — the <u>embryo</u> of a new organism.

2)   To start with, the <u>cells</u> in the embryo are <u>all the same</u>. They are called <u>embryonic stem cells</u>.

3)   These stem cells are able to <u>divide</u> to produce <u>different types</u> of <u>specialised cell</u>. For example, blood cells.

4)   The process of cells becoming specialised is called <u>differentiation</u>.

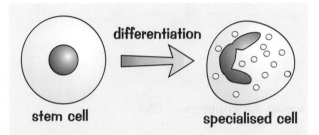

differentiation

stem cell   specialised cell

5)   In most <u>animal</u> cells, the ability to differentiate is <u>lost</u> at an early stage.

6)   <u>Adult</u> humans only have <u>stem cells</u> in certain places like <u>bone marrow</u> (the stuff inside your bones).

7)   Adult stem cells <u>aren't as useful</u> as the stem cells in embryos. This is because they can only differentiate into <u>certain types of cell</u>.

Stem Cells *May be Able to Cure Many Diseases*

1)   Doctors already use <u>adult stem cells</u> to cure some <u>diseases</u>.

2)   Scientists have experimented with <u>taking stem cells</u> from very early <u>human embryos</u> and <u>growing</u> them.

3)   Under certain conditions the stem cells will differentiate into <u>specialised cells</u>.

4)   It <u>might</u> be possible to create specialised cells to <u>replace</u> those which have been <u>damaged</u> by <u>disease</u> or <u>injury</u>.
For example, new <u>heart muscle cells</u> to help someone with <u>heart disease</u>.

5)   Before this can happen, a lot of <u>research</u> needs to be done.
There are many <u>ethical concerns</u> about stem cell research:

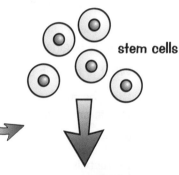

stem cells

new heart muscle cells

- Some people are strongly <u>against</u> embryonic stem cell research. They think that human embryos <u>shouldn't</u> be used for experiments because each one is a <u>potential human life</u>.
- Other people think that <u>curing patients</u> who are <u>suffering</u> is <u>more important</u> than the potential life of the embryos.
- In some countries stem cell research is <u>banned</u>. It's allowed in the UK under <u>strict guidelines</u>.

"She sells stem cells on the seashore" — try and say that really fast...

The <u>potential</u> of stem cells is <u>huge</u> — but it's <u>early days</u> yet and there are a lot of <u>ethical issues</u> to think about.

B2 Topic 1 — Genes and Enzymes

Revision Summary for B2 Topic 1

There's a lot to remember from this section. Some stuff like cloning and genetic engineering are hot topics. You need to know all sides of the story, as well as all the facts... So, here are some questions to help you figure out what you know. If you get any wrong, go back and learn the stuff.

1) Name two parts of a cell that both plants and animal cells have.

2) What three things do plant cells have that animal cells don't?

3) Name two features of a cell that bacteria have.

4)* A magnified image is 7.5 mm wide. The specimen is 0.3 mm wide. What is the magnification?

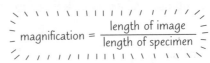

$$\text{magnification} = \frac{\text{length of image}}{\text{length of specimen}}$$

5) What shape is a molecule of DNA?

6) Name the four different bases found in DNA.

7) Name two scientists who had major roles in discovering the structure of DNA.

8) What is a gene?

9) Mutations are always harmful. True or False?

10) Give a definition of a catalyst.

11) In the 'lock and key mechanism', is the enzyme the lock or the key?

12) If you use iodine solution to test something with starch in it, what colour change will you see?

13)* This graph shows how enzyme activity depends on pH: State the optimum pH of the enzyme.

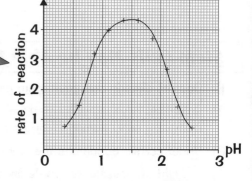

14) Give one advantage of genetic engineering.

15) Give one reason why some people are concerned about genetic engineering.

16) What is mitosis used for in the human body?

17) Strawberry plants form runners which become new plants. Is this an example of sexual or asexual reproduction?

18) Where does meiosis take place in the human body?

19) In meiosis:
a) How many cells are produced from the original cell?
b) Are the new cells diploid or haploid?

20) Give one possible use of cloning mammals.

21) Give one risk to do with trying to clone mammals.

22) What is meant by the 'differentiation' of cells?

23) Give one example of how embryonic stem cells could be used to cure diseases.

*Answers to these questions are given on p.108.

Respiration

Respiration is pretty important to life as we know it. So take a deep breath (sorry), and get stuck in...

Respiration *is NOT 'Breathing In and Out'*

Respiration is really important — it's how all living things get energy from food.

> RESPIRATION is the process of BREAKING DOWN GLUCOSE TO RELEASE ENERGY, which goes on IN EVERY LIVING CELL

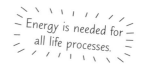

Energy is needed for all life processes.

Aerobic *Respiration Needs Plenty of* Oxygen

Aerobic respiration is respiration using oxygen. You need to learn the word equation for aerobic respiration:

> Glucose + Oxygen $\rightarrow$ Carbon Dioxide + Water (+ ENERGY)

Raw Materials *and* Waste Diffuse *In and Out of Cells*

1) Your circulatory system is made up of your heart and blood vessels. It carries glucose, oxygen (O_2) and carbon dioxide (CO_2) around the body in the blood.

2) The glucose needed for respiration comes from breaking down food in the digestive system.

3) The oxygen comes from air breathed into the lungs. Carbon dioxide is breathed out.

4) Capillaries are really tiny blood vessels. All cells have capillaries nearby to supply them with glucose and oxygen, and take away the waste carbon dioxide.

5) These substances move between the cells and the capillaries by a process called diffusion:

> DIFFUSION is the MOVEMENT OF PARTICLES from an area of HIGHER CONCENTRATION to an area of LOWER CONCENTRATION

- When cells respire, they use up O_2 and glucose.
- There's a higher concentration of O_2 and glucose in the blood than in the cells.
- So O_2 and glucose diffuse from the blood into the cells.

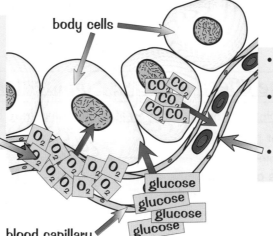

body cells

blood capillary

- When cells respire they produce lots of CO_2.
- There's a higher concentration of CO_2 in the cells than in the blood.
- So CO_2 diffuses from the cells into the blood.

Revision by diffusion — you wish...

Wouldn't that be great — if all this stuff would drift across, from an area of high concentration (in the book) to an area of low concentration (in your mind — no offence). Actually, it may just happen if you read it again...

Respiration and Exercise

Your rate of respiration (how fast you turn glucose into energy) depends on what you're doing...

When You Exercise You Respire More

1) Muscles need energy from respiration to contract.
2) When you exercise your muscles contract more often than normal, so you need more energy.
3) This energy comes from increased respiration.
4) The increase in respiration means you need to get more oxygen into the cells.
5) Your breathing rate increases to get more oxygen into the blood.
6) Your heart rate increases to get this oxygen around your body and to remove carbon dioxide more quickly.
7) When you do really hard exercise (like sprinting) your body can't supply oxygen to your muscles quickly enough. So they start respiring anaerobically (see below).

Learn this equation... and be able to use it: CARDIAC OUTPUT = HEART RATE × STROKE VOLUME

E.g. if you're told heart rate is 80 bpm and stroke volume is 70 cm³,
cardiac output = heart rate x stroke volume
= 80 x 70 = 5600 cm³ per min.

Cardiac output is the volume of blood the heart pumps in one minute — it increases as heart rate increases.

Anaerobic Respiration Doesn't Use Oxygen At All

1) Anaerobic respiration happens when there's not enough oxygen available. Here's the equation.

Glucose → Lactic Acid (+ ENERGY)

2) Anaerobic respiration does not release as much energy as aerobic respiration (but it's useful in emergencies).
3) It also produces a build-up of lactic acid in the muscles. This gets painful and can give you cramp.
4) The advantage of anaerobic respiration is that you can keep on using your muscles for a while longer.
5) But when you stop exercising, you'll have an oxygen debt.
6) In other words you have to 'repay' the oxygen which you didn't manage to get to your muscles in time. The amount of oxygen needed is called the excess post-exercise oxygen consumption (EPOC).
7) You have to keep breathing hard for a while after you stop exercising to get more oxygen into the blood.
8) Your heart rate stays high to get the oxygen to your muscles, where it's used to break down lactic acid.

You Can Look at the Effect of Exercise on Breathing and Heart Rate

1) You can measure breathing rate by counting breaths, and heart rate by taking the pulse.
2) E.g. you could take your pulse after:
   • sitting down for 5 minutes,
   • then after 5 minutes of jogging,
   • then again after running for 5 minutes,
   and plot your results in a bar chart.

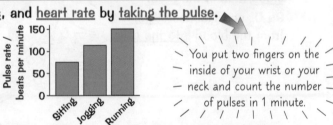

You put two fingers on the inside of your wrist or your neck and count the number of pulses in 1 minute.

3) Your pulse rate will increase the more intense (hard) the exercise is. This is because your body needs to get more oxygen to the muscles and take more carbon dioxide away from the muscles.

Oxygen debt — cheap to pay back...

Lots of brain power is needed for this page — it's quite a workout. Better get training (yep, I mean revising)...

Photosynthesis

You don't know photosynthesis 'til you know its <u>equation</u>. It's in a <u>nice green box</u> so you can't possibly miss it.

Plants *Make Their Own* Food *by Photosynthesis*

1) <u>Photosynthesis</u> is how <u>plants</u> produce '<u>food</u>'. This 'food' is <u>glucose</u>.
2) Photosynthesis happens in the leaves of all <u>green plants</u>.
3) Photosynthesis happens inside the <u>chloroplasts</u>.
4) <u>Chloroplasts</u> contain <u>chlorophyll</u>, which absorbs (takes in) <u>energy</u> in <u>sunlight</u>.
5) You need to learn the equation for photosynthesis:

$$\text{Carbon dioxide + water} \xrightarrow[\text{chlorophyll}]{\text{SUNLIGHT}} \text{glucose + oxygen}$$

Leaves *are Adapted for Photosynthesis*

1) Leaves are <u>broad</u>. This means there's a <u>large surface area</u> for <u>light</u> to fall on.
2) Leaves contain lots of <u>chlorophyll</u> in <u>chloroplasts</u> to <u>absorb light</u>.
3) Leaves are full of little holes called <u>stomata</u>. They open and close to let <u>carbon dioxide</u> in and <u>oxygen</u> out. They also allow <u>water vapour</u> to escape.

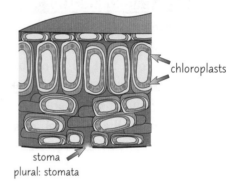

chloroplasts

stoma
plural: stomata

The *Limiting Factor for Photosynthesis Depends on the Conditions*

1) The rate of photosynthesis is affected by the <u>light</u> intensity, the concentration of <u>CO_2</u> and the <u>temperature</u>.
2) Any of these can become the <u>limiting factor</u> — the thing that stops photosynthesis going any <u>faster</u>.
3) Which factor is limiting at a particular time <u>changes</u>:
   - At <u>night</u> the limiting factor is <u>light</u>.
   - In <u>winter</u> it's often the <u>temperature</u>.
   - If it's warm and bright, the concentration of <u>carbon dioxide</u> is usually limiting.
4) You can do <u>experiments</u> to work out the <u>ideal conditions</u> for photosynthesis in a particular plant:

   - Measure the amount of <u>oxygen produced</u> in a given time (e.g. count the <u>bubbles</u> of oxygen given off by pondweed). This shows how <u>fast</u> photosynthesis is happening.
   - You can then <u>measure</u> how <u>different factors</u> change the <u>rate of photosynthesis</u> — see the next page...

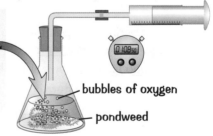

bubbles of oxygen

pondweed

If you don't do much revision, it's time to turn over a new leaf...

Another <u>word equation</u> for you... sorry. Oh, to have the life of a plant — constant sun-bathing and no exams...

The Rate of Photosynthesis

Before you start this page, make sure you've read the photosynthesis experiment on the last page...OK, go...

Three Important Graphs for Rate of Photosynthesis

① Not Enough LIGHT Slows Down the Rate of Photosynthesis

1) Light provides the energy needed for photosynthesis.

2) As the light level is raised, the rate of photosynthesis increases steadily — but only up to a certain point.

3) Beyond that, it won't make any difference. By then it'll be the temperature or the CO_2 level which is the limiting factor.

4) In the lab you can change the light intensity (amount of light) by moving a lamp closer to or further away from your plant.

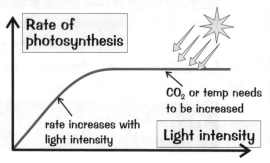

② Too Little CARBON DIOXIDE Also Slows it Down

1) Raising the CO_2 level increases the rate of photosynthesis.

2) But only up to a point — after this the graph flattens out. This shows that CO_2 is no longer the limiting factor.

3) As long as there's enough light and CO_2 then the limiting factor must be temperature.

4) To control the CO_2 level, dissolve different amounts of sodium hydrogen carbonate (which gives off CO_2) in the water.

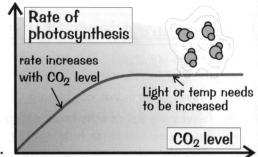

③ The TEMPERATURE has to be Just Right

1) If the temperature is the limiting factor it's usually because it's too low. The enzymes needed for photosynthesis work more slowly at low temperatures.

2) If the plant gets too hot, its enzymes will be denatured (destroyed). This happens at about 45 °C.

3) The best way to control the temperature of the flask in an experiment is to put it in a water bath.

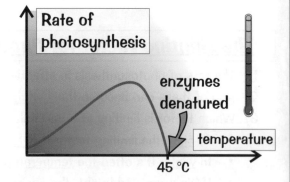

In all these experiments, you have to try and keep all the variables constant apart from the one you're investigating, so it's a fair test:

• use a bench lamp to control the intensity of the light

• keep the flask in a water bath to help keep the temperature constant

• use sodium hydrogen carbonate to control the level of CO_2, and make sure it's changed each time.

Don't blame it on the sunshine, don't blame it on the CO_2...

...don't blame it on the temperature, blame it on the plant. And now you'll never forget the three limiting factors in photosynthesis. No... well, make sure you read this page over and over again till you remember them all.

Osmosis

Osmosis. Oh my. Another fancy biology word to learn. Bet you can't wait to find out what it means...

Osmosis is Movement of Water Molecules Across a Membrane

OSMOSIS is the movement of water molecules across a partially permeable membrane from a region of high water concentration to a region of low water concentration.

1) A partially permeable membrane is just a membrane with very small holes in it.

2) The holes are so small that only tiny molecules (like water) can pass through them. Bigger molecules (like sugar) can't.

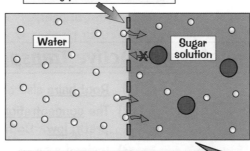

① When there are more water molecules on one side of a membrane than on the other...

The water molecules move both ways. But there's a net (overall) movement from one side to the other.

Partially permeable membrane

Water

Sugar solution

Net movement of water molecules

③ This movement of water means that the sugar solution gets more dilute.

The water acts like it's trying to "even up" the concentration either side of the membrane.

② ...there's a steady net flow of water into the side with fewer water molecules, i.e. into the sugar solution.

You Can do a Practical To Show Osmosis

1) Cut up a potato into identical cylinders.

2) Measure the lengths of the potato cylinders.

3) Get two beakers with different solutions in them:
   - One should be pure water.
   - One should be a sugar solution.

4) Then leave four cylinders in each beaker for half an hour.

5) After this, you take them out and measure their lengths again:
   - If water has moved into the cylinders by osmosis, they'll be a bit longer.
   - If water has moved out, they'll have shrunk a bit. What fun...

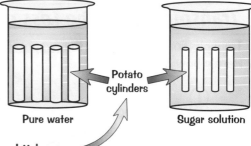

Potato cylinders

Pure water

Sugar solution

- The dependent variable in this practical is the length of the potato cylinder.
- The independent variable is the concentration of the sugar solution.
- To be a fair test all other variables (e.g. temperature, time, type of sugar) must be kept the same.

And to all you cold-hearted potato murderers...

The practical isn't much fun, but it helps you understand osmosis. Remember, water molecules move across a partially permeable membrane from a region of high water concentration to a region of low water concentration.

Water Uptake and Loss in Plants

If you don't water a house plant it goes all droopy, then it dies. The moral of this story — plants need water.

Root Hairs Take in Water by Osmosis

1) Roots have long 'hairs' which stick out into the soil.

2) Each root is covered in millions of teeny-tiny hairs.

3) This gives the plant a big surface area for absorbing water.

4) There's usually a high concentration of water in the soil. So the water enters the root hair cell by osmosis.

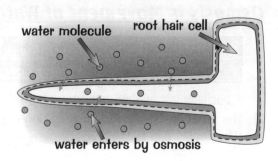

Root Hairs Take In Minerals Using Active Transport

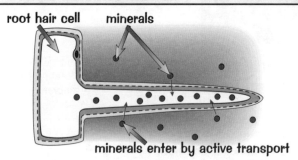

1) Root hairs also absorb minerals from the soil.

2) The concentration of minerals in the soil is usually pretty low. So normal diffusion doesn't work.

3) Instead a process called 'active transport' is used.

4) Active transport uses energy from respiration to help the plant pull minerals into the root hair. This happens against the concentration gradient.

Plants have tube networks. These move substances to and from individual cells quickly:

• XYLEM tubes transport water and minerals from the root to the rest of the plant (e.g. the leaves).

• PHLOEM tubes transport sugars from the leaves (where they're made) to growing and storage tissues.

Transpiration is the Loss of Water from the Plant

Transpiration is caused by the evaporation and diffusion of water from inside the leaves. Here's how it happens:

Evaporation is when water turns from a liquid into a gas.

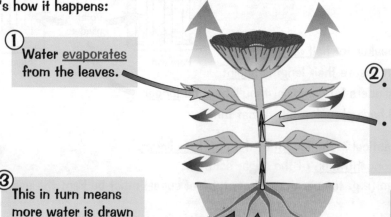

① Water evaporates from the leaves.

② • This creates a slight shortage of water in the leaf.

• More water is drawn up from the rest of the plant through the xylem vessels to replace it.

③ This in turn means more water is drawn up from the roots.

This means there's a constant stream of water through the plant. This is called the transpiration stream.

If you think revision is thirsty work — try being a plant...

Plants lose so much water that they need to take in loads. That's why they have all those root hairs, you see...*

* not because they can't be bothered to shave.

Distribution — Pooters and Pitfall Traps

Looking at <u>distribution</u> gives you the chance to <u>rummage around</u> in bushes and look at some <u>real organisms</u>...

Organisms Live in Different Places

1) A <u>habitat</u> is the place where an organism <u>lives</u>, e.g. a playing field.

2) The <u>distribution</u> of an organism is <u>where</u> an organism is <u>found</u>, e.g. in a part of the playing field.

3) To <u>study</u> the distribution of an organism, you can <u>measure</u> how common an organism is in <u>two sample areas</u>. Then you can compare your results for the two areas.

4) There are various ways to <u>measure</u> how common an organism is...

Pooters Are For Collecting Ground Insects

<u>Pooters</u> are jars that have rubber bungs sealing the top, and <u>two tubes</u> stuck through the bung. Like this one:

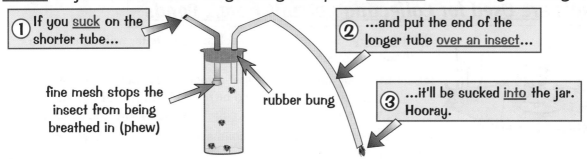

① If you <u>suck</u> on the shorter tube...

② ...and put the end of the longer tube <u>over an insect</u>...

③ ...it'll be sucked <u>into</u> the jar. Hooray.

fine mesh stops the insect from being breathed in (phew)

rubber bung

1) In your <u>first sample area</u>, crawl around for a <u>few minutes</u> sucking up as many insects as you can.

2) Then <u>count</u> the number of insects you've collected.

3) Do this in your <u>second</u> sample area and <u>compare</u> what you find.

4) Spend the <u>same</u> amount of <u>time</u> sampling in each area, and choose sample areas of a <u>similar size</u>.

Pitfall Traps Are Another Way to Study Ground Insects

<u>Pitfall traps</u> are <u>steep-sided pots</u>. They're sunk in a <u>hole</u> in the ground with the top <u>partly open</u>. Like this:

① Leave the trap <u>overnight</u> in your <u>first sample</u> area.

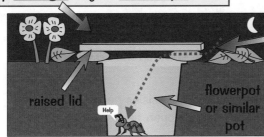

② Insects that come along <u>fall</u> into the container and <u>can't get out</u> again. So you can <u>count</u> them.

raised lid

Help

flowerpot or similar pot

Then set up a pitfall trap in your <u>second</u> <u>sample</u> area and <u>compare</u> what you find.

Traps have their pitfalls and pooters really suck...

For these experiments, you should <u>repeat</u> the measurements <u>several times</u> and then take the <u>average</u> result. But setting up a pitfall trap the <u>same way</u> over and over again is a lot more <u>tricky</u> than doing a regular lab experiment.

Distribution — Nets and Quadrats

I don't know about you but I just can't get enough of <u>collecting insects</u>...

Sweep Nets are Used for Collecting Animals from Long Grass

1) A <u>sweep net</u> is a net lined with <u>strong cloth</u>. It's used for collecting insects, spiders, etc. from <u>long grass</u>.

2) To use one, <u>stand still</u> in your first sample area. Sweep the net <u>once</u> from <u>left to right</u> through the grass. Then <u>quickly</u> turn the insects out into a <u>container</u> to <u>count</u> them.

3) <u>Repeat</u> the sweep in your second sample area. Then <u>compare</u> what you find.

Pond Nets are Used for Collecting Animals from... Ponds

1) A <u>pond net</u> is a net used for collecting insects, water snails, etc. from <u>ponds</u> and <u>rivers</u>.

2) To use one, stand in your first sample area. Sweep the net <u>along the bottom</u> of the pond or river. Turn the net out into a <u>white tray</u> with a bit of water in to <u>count</u> the organisms you've caught.

3) Then do a sweep in your second sample area. <u>Compare</u> what you find.

Use a Quadrat to Study The Distribution of Small Organisms

A <u>quadrat</u> is a <u>square</u> frame enclosing a <u>known area</u>, e.g. 1 m². To compare <u>how common</u> an organism is in <u>two sample areas</u>, follow these steps:

A quadrat

1) Place a <u>1 m² quadrat</u> on the ground at a <u>random point</u> within the <u>first</u> sample area.

> It's really important it's random — if all your samples are in <u>one spot</u> and everywhere else is <u>different</u>, the results you get won't be <u>reproducible</u>.

2) <u>Count</u> all the organisms you're interested in <u>within</u> the quadrat.

3) <u>Repeat</u> steps 1 and 2 lots of times. (The larger the <u>sample size</u> the better.)

4) <u>Work out</u> the <u>mean</u> number of organisms per quadrat within the first sample area.

5) <u>Repeat</u> steps 1-4 in the <u>second</u> sample area.

6) Finally <u>compare</u> the two means. E.g. you might find 2 daisies per m² in the shade, and 22 daisies per m² (lots more) in an open field.

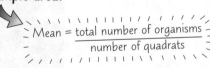

Mean = $\dfrac{\text{total number of organisms}}{\text{number of quadrats}}$

Drat, drat, and double drat — my favourite use of quadrats...

<u>Quadrats</u> are really <u>handy</u> for studying <u>distribution</u>. Not that it's what I spend my weekends doing or anything...

More on Distribution

If this page makes no sense, <u>turn back</u>. Turn back two pages, I mean, not turn back and abandon all hope...

Population Size *is the* Number of Organisms *in a* Population

To work out the <u>population size</u> of an organism in one sample area:

1) Work out the <u>mean number of organisms per m²</u>. If your quadrat has an area of 1 m² then it's just the same calculation as the last page.

Mean = total number of organisms / number of quadrats

2) Next, work out the <u>total area</u> of the sample area — multiply the <u>length</u> by the <u>width</u>.

3) Then multiply the <u>mean</u> by the <u>total area</u> (in m²) of the habitat.

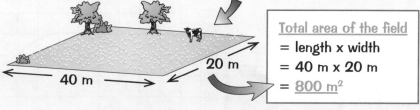

For example, a field measures <u>40 m</u> by <u>20 m</u>.

The <u>mean</u> number of daisies per m² is <u>22</u>.

40 m   20 m

Total area of the field
= length x width
= 40 m x 20 m
= <u>800 m²</u>

The size of the daisy <u>population</u> = the <u>mean</u> x the <u>total area</u>
= 22 x 800 = <u>17 600 daisies</u>.

You can also find out how the <u>distribution</u> of an organism <u>gradually changes</u> across an area (e.g. from a hedge to the middle of a field). You can do this using a <u>belt transect</u>:

1) <u>Mark out a line</u> in the area you want to study.

2) Put a quadrat down at the <u>start</u> of the <u>line</u> and <u>count</u> your organisms.

3) Then, take samples by <u>moving</u> your quadrat <u>along the line</u>.

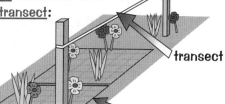

transect

quadrat

You Need to Know How to *Measure Environmental Factors*

1) You might find there's a <u>difference</u> in the <u>distribution</u> of organisms.

2) So then you can investigate the <u>environmental factors</u> that <u>might</u> be <u>causing</u> this difference.

- For example, if you found that <u>daisies</u> were more common in one area than the other, you could measure the <u>light intensity</u> in both places.
- You'd probably find that the light is much <u>brighter</u> in the area with more daisies.
- One reason <u>could</u> be that there are more daisies because they get <u>more sunlight</u> for <u>photosynthesis</u>.

3) Here's how you can <u>measure</u> some <u>environmental factors</u>:

- Use a <u>thermometer</u> to measure the <u>temperature</u> in different places.
- Use an electronic device called a <u>light sensor</u> to measure <u>light intensity</u>.
- Measure <u>soil pH</u> using an <u>electronic pH monitor</u>.

Scientists are easily amused — just stick them in a field with a quadrat...

Being able to <u>work out</u> the <u>population size</u> of an organism in a sample area is pretty <u>useful</u>. After all, it would take quite a while to count 17 600 daisies. What's more, examiners love it, so make sure you <u>know how to do it</u>...

Revision Summary for B2 Topic 2

Hurrah. The section is almost complete. Before you move on to Topic 3, try these revision questions. Do them all and check your answers. If you get any wrong, then learn those bits again, and do the questions again. Keep on going until you can get all the questions right. It's a hard slog, but you've got to do it. Otherwise all the useful facts you've just read will float away... and you'll be left with nothing but a mental image of an ant in a plant pot.

1) Which of the following statements are true?
   a) Respiration is breathing in and out.
   b) Carbon dioxide is made in aerobic respiration.

2) What is diffusion?

3) Write down the word equation for anaerobic respiration.

4) Give one disadvantage of anaerobic respiration.

5)* Danny measured his heart rate before, during and after exercise. He plotted a graph of the results.
   a) What was Danny's heart rate (in beats per minute) when he was at rest (before exercising)?
   b) What was Danny's highest heart rate?

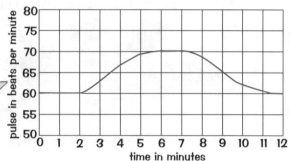

6) What is the green substance in leaves that absorbs energy from sunlight?

7) Write down the equation for photosynthesis.

8) Name one of the three factors that can limit photosynthesis.

9) Explain why it's important that a plant doesn't get too hot.

10) What is osmosis?

11) A solution of pure water is separated from a sugar solution by a partially permeable membrane. The net flow of water molecules across the membrane will be in the direction of the pure water. True or False?

12) What is the advantage to a plant of having root hairs?

13) Xylem tubes transport water and minerals. True or False?

14) Describe how you collect insects using a pooter.

15) Say you are investigating the population of an organism in a field. Should you place your quadrat randomly or where you can see most of the organism you are studying?

16)* The total area of a garden is 200 m². The mean number of gnomes per m² is 5. What is the size of the gnome population in the garden?

population size = mean × total area

17) How do you measure soil pH?

18) Are you having fun revising?

*Answers to these questions are given on p.108.

Evidence for Evolution

THEORY OF EVOLUTION: More than 3 billion years ago, life on Earth began as simple organisms from which all the more complex organisms evolved.

Fossils Provide Lots of Evidence for Evolution

1) A fossil is <u>any trace</u> of an animal or plant that lived long ago.

2) Fossils can be <u>formed</u> in three ways:

① From <u>impressions</u> that have been left in <u>soft materials</u> like clay. E.g. footprints.

② From the <u>hard bits</u> of animals that <u>don't easily decay</u>. E.g. teeth, bones and shells.

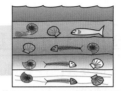

③ From parts of organisms that <u>don't decay</u> because the <u>conditions aren't right</u> for microbes to work. E.g. in amber (where there's no oxygen or moisture.)

Microbes are tiny organisms, (e.g. bacteria) that can break down things.

Fossils Found in Rock Layers Tell Us Three Things:

1) What the creatures and plants <u>looked like</u>.

2) How <u>long ago</u> they existed. Generally, the <u>deeper</u> the rock, the <u>older</u> the fossil.

3) How they've <u>evolved</u>. From looking at fossils in rocks of different ages, we can see how species have <u>changed</u> over <u>billions of years</u>.

The Fossil Record is Incomplete

There are <u>gaps</u> in the fossil record. This is because:

1) <u>Very few</u> dead plants or animals actually turn into fossils. Most just <u>decay away</u>.

2) Some body parts, like <u>soft tissue</u>, tend to decay away <u>completely</u>.

3) There are fossils <u>yet to be found</u> that might help complete the picture.

A fossil record — try my dad's CD collection...

You need to learn how <u>fossils</u> provide <u>evidence</u> for <u>evolution</u> and why there are <u>gaps</u> in the <u>fossil record</u>. Then, for some revision relief, make a cuppa or have a <u>dig in the garden</u> — you never know what you might find...

Growth and Development

Growth is pretty <u>important</u>. Without it, you wouldn't be able to reach anything on the top shelf...

Growth *is an Increase in Size or Mass (Weight)*

You can <u>measure</u> the <u>growth</u> of an organism in these three ways:

1) `Size` — You can measure its <u>height</u>, <u>length</u>, <u>width</u> or <u>circumference</u>.

2) `Wet mass` — This is the mass <u>including all the water</u> in an organism's body. It can <u>vary</u> a lot.

3) `Dry mass` — This is the mass of an organism when it's <u>dead</u> and has been <u>dried out</u>.

The circumference is the width around an object

Plants *and* Animals Grow Differently

Plants and animals <u>grow</u> and <u>develop</u> due to these processes:

1) <u>CELL DIFFERENTIATION</u> — the process where a cell <u>changes</u> to become <u>specialised</u> for its <u>job</u>.

2) <u>CELL DIVISION</u> — by <u>mitosis</u>.

3) <u>CELL ELONGATION</u> — where a plant cell <u>expands</u>, making the cell <u>bigger</u> and so making the plant <u>grow</u>. It happens only in <u>plants</u>.

Growth in animals...
• Happens by <u>cell division</u>.
• Animals tend to <u>grow</u> while they're <u>young</u> then reach full growth and <u>stop</u> growing.
• Once you're an adult, most cell division is for <u>repair</u> — to <u>replace</u> old or damaged cells.
• <u>Cell differentiation</u> is <u>lost</u> at an <u>early stage</u>.

Growth in plants...
• Happens all the time. Plants <u>differentiate</u> to <u>develop new parts</u>, e.g. leaves, roots.
• Growth in <u>height</u> is mainly due to <u>cell elongation</u>.
• Cell <u>division</u> usually just happens in the <u>tips</u> of the <u>roots</u> and <u>shoots</u>.

Percentile Charts *show* Growth Data

<u>Growth charts</u> are used to check that babies and children are <u>growing normally</u>. For example:

- A baby's growth (e.g. mass) is <u>plotted</u> on an <u>average growth chart</u>.
- The chart shows a number of '<u>percentiles</u>'. E.g. the <u>50th percentile</u> shows the mass that <u>50%</u> of babies will have reached at a certain age.
- This chart shows a one-year-old who weighs <u>10 kg</u> is in the <u>75th percentile</u>. This means 75% of one-year-olds are lighter and 25% are heavier.
- Babies <u>vary</u> in size. Doctors aren't usually concerned unless a baby's size is above the <u>98th</u> percentile or below the <u>2nd</u> percentile.

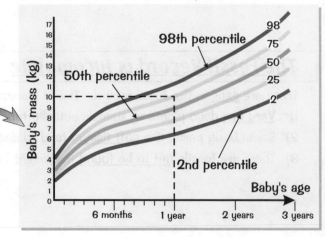

I'm growing rather sick of this topic...

<u>Growth data</u> is pretty dull, but <u>you've got to know it</u>. Definitely below the 2nd percentile in terms of enjoyment.*

*This means 98% of things are more fun. Sorry...

Cell Organisation and the Circulatory System

Cells are organised. This involves a to-do list, a diary and a nice big spreadsheet...

Cells Make Up Tissues, Organs and Systems

1) Cells differentiate to become specialised.
2) Specialised cells form tissues, which form organs, which form organ systems:

- A tissue (e.g. muscle tissue) is a group of similar cells that work together to carry out a particular function.
- An organ (e.g. the heart) is a group of different tissues that work together to perform a particular function.
- An organ system (e.g. the circulatory system) is a group of organs working together to perform a function.

The Heart is Part of the Circulatory System

The heart has four chambers — the left atrium, the right atrium, the left ventricle and the right ventricle.
It also has four major blood vessels — the vena cava, the pulmonary artery, the pulmonary vein and the aorta.

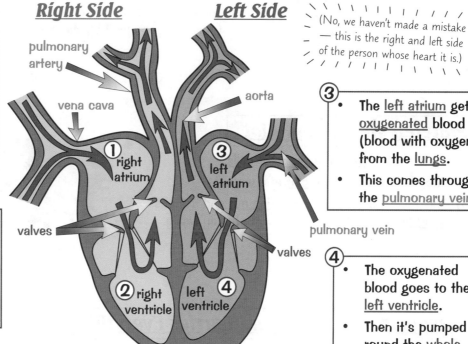

Right Side　　**Left Side**

(No, we haven't made a mistake — this is the right and left side of the person whose heart it is.)

① • The right atrium gets deoxygenated blood (blood without oxygen) from the body.
　• This comes through the vena cava.

② • The deoxygenated blood goes to the right ventricle.
　• Then it's pumped to the lungs (via the pulmonary artery).

③ • The left atrium gets oxygenated blood (blood with oxygen) from the lungs.
　• This comes through the pulmonary vein.

④ • The oxygenated blood goes to the left ventricle.
　• Then it's pumped round the whole body via the aorta.

pulmonary artery
vena cava
aorta
right atrium
left atrium
valves
pulmonary vein
valves
② right ventricle
④ left ventricle

SPECIAL FEATURES OF THE HEART

1) The left ventricle has a much thicker wall than the right ventricle. It has more muscle because it needs to pump blood around the whole body, not just to the lungs.
2) The heart has valves. Valves prevent the backflow of blood.

Soft and quilted — the best kind of tissues...

So, cells form tissues, tissues form organs, and organs form organ systems. I wish I was that neat and tidy...

The Circulatory System — The Blood

The heart's a bit obsessed with pumping <u>blood</u> — it must be important stuff. Blood contains <u>four main things</u>...

Red Blood Cells Carry Oxygen

1) The job of red blood cells is to carry <u>oxygen</u> from the lungs to all the cells in the body.

2) Red blood cells have a doughnut (or '<u>biconcave disc</u>') shape. This gives them a <u>large surface area</u> for absorbing (taking in) <u>oxygen</u>.

3) Red blood cells contain a substance called <u>haemoglobin</u>.

4) Haemoglobin is the stuff that allows red blood cells to <u>carry oxygen</u>.

5) Red blood cells <u>don't</u> have a nucleus — this allows more room for haemoglobin.

White Blood Cells Defend Against Disease

1) They can change shape to gobble up <u>microorganisms</u>.

2) They produce <u>antibodies</u> to fight microorganisms.

3) They also produce <u>antitoxins</u> to get rid of any toxins (poisons) produced by the microorganisms.

Platelets Help Blood Clot

1) Platelets are <u>small fragments</u> of <u>cells</u>.

2) They help the blood to <u>clot</u> at a wound.

3) This stops all your <u>blood pouring out</u> and it stops <u>microorganisms</u> getting in. Pretty handy really.

Plasma is the Liquid That Carries Everything in Blood

Plasma is a liquid which keeps the blood <u>fluid</u>. It <u>carries</u> just about <u>everything</u>, including:

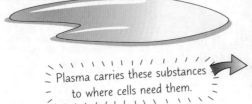

Plasma carries these substances to where cells need them.

1) <u>Red</u> and <u>white blood cells</u>, and <u>platelets</u>.

2) <u>Antibodies</u> and <u>antitoxins</u> produced by the white blood cells.

3) <u>Hormones</u>.

4) Nutrients like <u>glucose</u> and <u>amino acids</u>.

5) <u>Waste products</u> like <u>carbon dioxide</u> and <u>urea</u> (wee).

Platelets — ideal for small dinners...

<u>Blood</u> is a bit of a wonder liquid. It's jam packed <u>full of useful things</u> — so it can <u>fight diseases</u> and <u>stop</u> you <u>bleeding</u>. Plus it carries <u>oxygen</u> and loads of <u>important substances</u> around your body. It's pretty awesome stuff.

The Circulatory System — Blood Vessels

The circulatory system needs <u>blood vessels</u> to <u>transport</u> the blood. It all gets a bit messy otherwise.

Blood Vessels are Designed for Their Function

There are <u>three</u> different types of <u>blood vessel</u>:

1) <u>ARTERIES</u> — these carry the blood <u>away</u> from the heart.
2) <u>CAPILLARIES</u> — these are involved in the <u>exchange of materials</u> with the tissues.
3) <u>VEINS</u> — these carry the blood <u>to</u> the heart.

Arteries Carry Blood Under Pressure

1) The artery walls are <u>strong</u> and <u>elastic</u>.
2) This is because the heart pumps blood out at <u>high pressure</u>.
3) The walls are <u>thick</u>. The hole in the middle is <u>small</u>.
4) The walls have thick layers of <u>muscle</u> to make them <u>strong</u>.

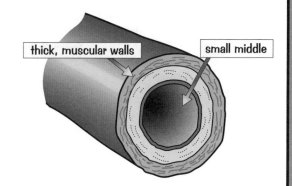

thick, muscular walls

small middle

Capillaries are Really Small

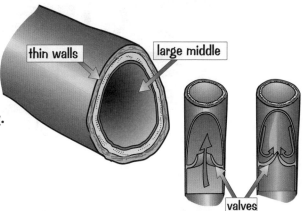

thin wall — only one cell thick

nucleus of cell

1) Arteries branch into <u>capillaries</u>.
2) Capillaries are really <u>tiny</u> — too small to see.
3) They carry the blood <u>really close</u> to <u>every cell</u> in the body to <u>exchange substances</u> with them.
4) They have <u>permeable</u> walls. This means substances can <u>diffuse</u> in and out.
5) They supply <u>food</u> and <u>oxygen</u>, and take away <u>wastes</u> like <u>carbon dioxide</u>.
6) Their walls are usually <u>only one cell thick</u>. This means that substances can <u>diffuse in and out quickly</u>, because they only have a <u>small distance</u> to cross.

Veins Take Blood Back to the Heart

1) Capillaries <u>join up</u> to form <u>veins</u>.
2) The walls of veins are <u>thinner</u> than artery walls.
3) This is because blood is at <u>lower pressure</u> in the veins.
4) Their middle is <u>bigger</u> than arteries to help the blood <u>flow</u>.
5) Veins also have <u>valves</u>. These help keep the blood flowing in the <u>right direction</u>.

thin walls

large middle

valves

Learn this page — don't struggle in vein...

You need to <u>learn</u> the <u>differences</u> between the different types of blood vessel. Remember... <u>a</u>rteries carry blood <u>a</u>way from the heart. <u>C</u>apillaries are one <u>c</u>ell thick so stuff can easily <u>c</u>ross their walls. And <u>v</u>eins have <u>v</u>alves.

Peristalsis and Digestive Enzymes

Food. Yum. It has a happy journey from mouth to stomach, being broken down by enzymes along the way.

Peristalsis Moves Food Along the Gut

1) There's muscular tissue all the way down your gut — there are:
   - longitudinal muscles down the length of the gut
   - circular muscles running in circles around the gut.
2) These muscles contract (get tighter) to squeeze the food along.
3) This squeezing action is called peristalsis.

The gut is also called the alimentary canal.

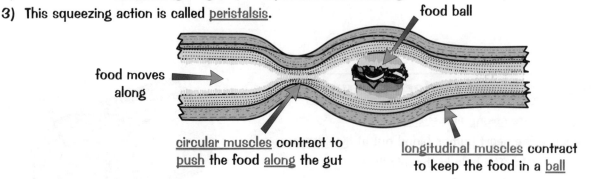

food ball

food moves along

circular muscles contract to push the food along the gut

longitudinal muscles contract to keep the food in a ball

Food is Broken Down by Enzymes

1) Starch, proteins and fats are BIG molecules — too big to pass through the walls of the gut.
2) Sugars, amino acids, glycerol and fatty acids are much smaller molecules. They can pass easily through the walls of the gut.
3) The digestive enzymes break down the BIG molecules into the smaller ones.

Big molecules like starch are insoluble (don't dissolve in water). They're broken down into smaller molecules like sugars, which are soluble (do dissolve in water).

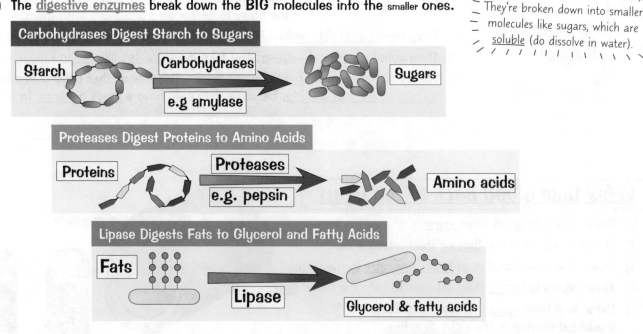

Carbohydrases Digest Starch to Sugars

Starch → Carbohydrases e.g amylase → Sugars

Proteases Digest Proteins to Amino Acids

Proteins → Proteases e.g. pepsin → Amino acids

Lipase Digests Fats to Glycerol and Fatty Acids

Fats → Lipase → Glycerol & fatty acids

Peristalsis — useful for when you want to eat upside down...

Enzymes break down big molecules into smaller ones so you can absorb them. Handy. And peristalsis — muscle contractions which squeeze food along the gut. Lovely. Perhaps not one to mention at the dinner table...

The Digestive System

Digestive enzymes are produced in <u>various places</u> in your digestive system...

Food is Broken Down as it Goes Through the Gut

Mouth

1) Food is <u>moistened</u> with <u>saliva</u>.

2) Saliva contains <u>amylase</u>, which breaks down starch.

3) Food is <u>chewed</u> to form a <u>ball of food</u>. Then it's <u>swallowed</u>.

Tongue

Oesophagus

1) This is the tube that takes food from the <u>mouth</u> to the <u>stomach</u>.

2) It's lined with <u>muscles</u>. These <u>contract</u> to help the ball of food move along, by <u>peristalsis</u> (see page 38).

Liver

Produces <u>bile</u>. (Bile helps <u>digest fats</u>.)

Stomach

1) It <u>pummels</u> the food with its muscular walls.

2) It produces the <u>protease</u> enzyme, <u>pepsin</u>.

3) It produces <u>hydrochloric acid</u> for two reasons:
   a) To <u>kill bacteria</u>
   b) To give the <u>right pH</u> for the <u>protease</u> enzyme to work (pH 2 — <u>acidic</u>).

Small Intestine

1) Produces <u>protease</u>, <u>amylase</u> and <u>lipase</u> enzymes.

2) This is also where the "food" is <u>absorbed</u> into the body.

Pancreas

1) Produces <u>protease</u>, <u>amylase</u> and <u>lipase</u> enzymes.

2) It releases these into the <u>small intestine</u>.

Large Intestine

Where <u>excess water</u> is <u>absorbed</u> from the food.

There's something for you to chew on...

Peckish? Go and make a <u>sandwich</u> and while you tuck in, think about the <u>enzyme party</u> going on in your <u>gut</u>...

Investigating Digestive Enzymes

You can investigate the effect of <u>different concentrations</u> of a digestive enzyme on its substrate — what fun...

Use Visking Tubing to Model the Gut

1) Visking tubing is a <u>good model</u> for the gut. Like the gut, it lets <u>small molecules</u> through it but <u>not big ones</u>. It's also <u>cheaper</u>, <u>easier</u> and <u>less yukky</u> than using an animal's gut.

2) However, your gut's <u>longer</u> and has a <u>massive surface area</u>. This means the <u>speed</u> of digestion and absorption will be slightly <u>different</u>.

Use Iodine to Test for Starch and Benedict's to Test for Sugar

You can look at the effect of <u>amylase</u> concentrations on the digestion of <u>starch</u>. You do it like this...

1) Add the <u>same volume</u> of <u>starch suspension</u> and <u>0.25% amylase solution</u> to the visking tubing.

2) <u>Rinse</u> the outside of the tubing and put it into <u>distilled water</u>.

3) <u>Straight away</u> test a drop of <u>water</u> from around the tubing with <u>iodine solution</u> (see p.15) and with <u>Benedict's reagent</u>. Record the <u>colour</u>.

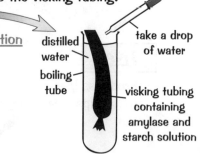

distilled water

boiling tube

take a drop of water

visking tubing containing amylase and starch solution

> **USING BENEDICT'S REAGENT:**
> Benedict's reagent starts off blue and will change colour if there's any sugar present.
>
> blue → green → yellow → orange → brick-red
>
> The more sugar there is, the further the colour change goes towards brick-red.

4) Then test the water again <u>after 15 minutes</u>. Record the <u>colour</u> each time.

5) <u>Repeat</u> the experiment using <u>other concentrations</u> of the amylase solution, e.g. 0.5%, 1.0%, etc.

6) You might get <u>results</u> like this...

Amylase concentration	Colour of iodine solution		Colour of Benedict's reagent	
	start of experiment	end of experiment	start of experiment	end of experiment
0.25%	orangey-brown	orangey-brown	blue	yellow
0.5%	orangey-brown	orangey-brown	blue	orange
1%	orangey-brown	orangey-brown	blue	brick-red

Keep everything except the amylase concentration <u>constant</u>.

- This colour shows that there's <u>no starch</u> in the water.
- This is because the starch molecules are <u>too big</u> to pass through the visking tubing.

- This colour shows that there's <u>sugar</u> in the water.
- This is because <u>starch</u> has been <u>broken down</u> by <u>amylase</u> to <u>sugar</u>. The sugar molecules are <u>small enough</u> to pass through the membrane into the water.

Enzyme Concentration Affects the Rate of Reaction

1) The <u>higher</u> the concentration of <u>amylase</u>, the <u>faster the rate of reaction</u>.

2) This is because the <u>more amylase</u> there is, the <u>faster</u> it <u>breaks down the starch</u>.

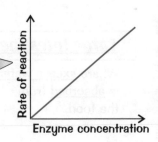

Rate of reaction

Enzyme concentration

The higher your concentration, the faster the rate of revision...

This is a fairly <u>grim</u> experiment, but at least you get some <u>pretty colours</u>. Learn all of this page in all its glory.

Functional Foods

Not all bacteria are bad — there are <u>friendly</u> ones too which help you out with <u>digestion</u>. Ahh, cheers guys...

Functional Foods **are Said to have** Health Benefits

A <u>functional food</u> is one that has some kind of <u>health benefit</u> beyond basic <u>nutrition</u>. For example:

① Probiotics **Contain** 'Good' Bacteria

1) Probiotics are <u>live bacteria</u>, such as *Bifidobacteria* and *Lactobacillus* (a lactic acid bacterium). These 'good bacteria' are similar to those that are found <u>naturally</u> in your <u>gut</u>.
2) Probiotics are added to foods like <u>yogurt</u>.
3) It's thought that they help to keep your <u>digestive system healthy</u> and your <u>immune system strong</u>. (Your immune system protects you against disease.)

② Prebiotics **Promote the** Growth **of** 'Good' Bacteria

1) Prebiotics are <u>carbohydrates</u> that we can't digest, e.g. <u>oligosaccharides</u>.
2) They are found <u>naturally</u> in foods like <u>leeks</u> and <u>onions</u>.
3) Some people take prebiotic <u>supplements</u> (extra prebiotics).
4) Prebiotics are a <u>food supply</u> for the <u>'good' bacteria</u> that are already in your gut.
5) It's thought that prebiotics help the 'good' bacteria <u>grow</u> in the <u>gut</u>. This could improve your <u>digestive and immune systems</u>.

③ Plant Stanol Esters Reduce Cholesterol

1) <u>Plant stanol esters</u> are chemicals that can <u>lower blood cholesterol</u> and reduce the risk of <u>heart disease</u>.
2) Stanols <u>occur naturally</u> in plants.
3) Some food manufacturers add them to <u>spreads</u>. People who are worried about their blood <u>cholesterol</u> levels may choose these spreads over normal spreads.

Not All Health Claims **are Scientifically Proven**

Functional foods <u>claim</u> they have certain <u>health benefits</u>. But how do you know they work... Well, when looking at evidence, it's a good idea to <u>watch out</u> for <u>these things</u>:

> - Is the report a SCIENTIFIC STUDY, published in a well-known science journal?
> - Was it written by a QUALIFIED PERSON, who doesn't work for the people selling the product?
> - Did the study ask a LARGE ENOUGH SAMPLE of people to give reliable results?
> - Have there been OTHER STUDIES which have found similar results?

A "yes" to one or more of these is a good sign.

E.g. A study in <u>The New England Journal of Medicine</u> provided evidence that <u>plant stanols</u> lower <u>blood cholesterol</u>. The study was in a <u>well-known science journal</u> and there have been <u>other studies</u> that have found <u>similar results</u>. Both of these suggest the study is <u>reliable</u>.

While you're in there, make yourself useful...

Don't get functional foods mixed up — <u>pr</u>obiotics are bacteria you eat to 'top up' the bacteria in your gut. Prebiotics are non-digestable carbohydrates that <u>fee</u>d the 'good' bacteria. And stan<u>o</u>ls are all about cholester<u>o</u>l.

Revision Summary for B2 Topic 3

And where do you think you're going? It's no use just reading through and thinking you've got it all —
this stuff will only stick in your head if you've learnt it <u>properly</u>. And that's what these questions are for.

I won't pretend they'll be easy — they're not meant to be, but all the information's in the section somewhere.
Have a go at all the questions, then if there are any you can't answer, go back, look stuff up and try again.
Enjoy...

1)   What is a fossil?

2)   Give one reason why the fossil record is incomplete.

3)   What is wet mass?

4)   Give one difference between growth in animals and growth in plants.

5)   What are growth charts used for?

6)   What is a tissue? What about an organ?

7)   Why does the left ventricle have a thicker wall than the right ventricle?

8)   Why does the heart have valves?

9)   What do you call the stuff in red blood cells that carries oxygen?

10) List two things that white blood cells produce.

11) Name three substance that get carried around the body in plasma.

12) Why do arteries have strong, elastic walls?

13) Why do capillaries have really thin walls?

14) Muscles contract to squeeze food along the gut. What is this squeezing action called?

15) What do carbohydrases do?

16) What two products does lipase break down fats into?

17) Why does the stomach produce hydrochloric acid?

18) What is the function of the small intestine?

19) In a digestive enzyme experiment, what could you use to model the gut?

20) What can you use to test if sugar is present in a solution?

21) What are prebiotics? Why might some people choose to take them as a supplement?

22) Why are plant stanol esters added to spreads?

23) Give two things you should look out for when deciding whether a health claim about a functional food
     is true or not.

Atoms

Atoms are the building blocks of <u>everything</u> — and they're <u>really, really tiny</u>.

Atoms have a Small *Nucleus* Surrounded by *Electrons*

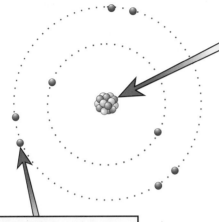

The Nucleus

1) It's in the <u>middle</u> of the atom.
2) It's <u>tiny</u> compared to the rest of the atom.
3) It contains <u>protons</u> and <u>neutrons</u>.
4) <u>Protons</u> are <u>positively (+) charged</u>.
5) <u>Neutrons</u> have <u>no charge</u> (they're neutral).

The Electrons

1) Move <u>around</u> the nucleus.
2) They're <u>negatively (−) charged</u>.
3) They move in <u>shells</u> (energy levels) around the nucleus.

Know Your *Particles...*

PARTICLE	RELATIVE MASS	CHARGE
Proton	1	+1
Neutron	1	0
Electron	almost nothing	−1

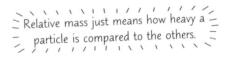

Relative mass just means how heavy a particle is compared to the others.

Number of Protons *Equals* Number of Electrons

1) Atoms have <u>no charge</u> overall. They're neutral.
2) The <u>charge</u> on the <u>electrons</u> is the <u>same</u> size as the charge on the <u>protons</u> — but <u>opposite</u>.
3) This means the <u>number of protons</u> always <u>equals</u> the <u>number of electrons</u> in an <u>atom</u>.

Basic atom facts — they don't take up much space...

Atoms are <u>tiny</u>. But the atom's <u>nucleus</u> is <u>REALLY</u> tiny. If you imagine a whole atom as the size of a <u>football stadium</u>, its <u>nucleus</u> would only be the size of a <u>marble</u>. Wow. That's little.

Electron Shells

The fact that electrons hang out in "shells" around the nucleus is what causes the whole of chemistry.

Electron Shell Rules:

1) Electrons always move in shells (sometimes called energy levels).

2) The inner shells are always filled first — these are the ones closest to the nucleus.

3) Only a certain number of electrons are allowed in each shell:
   1st shell: 2   2nd shell: 8   3rd shell: 8

4) Atoms are much happier when they have full electron shells.

5) In most atoms the outer shell is not full and this makes the atom want to react to fill it.

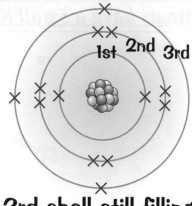

1st 2nd 3rd

3rd shell still filling

Follow the Rules to Work Out Electronic Configurations

You need to know the electronic configurations for the first 20 elements. For a quick example, take nitrogen. Follow the steps...

Electronic configuration means how many electrons are in each shell.

1) A nitrogen atom has seven protons... so it must have seven electrons.

2) Follow the 'Electron Shell Rules' above. The first shell can only take 2 electrons and the second shell can take a maximum of 8 electrons.

3) So the electronic configuration for nitrogen must be 2, 5. Easy peasy.

4) Now you try it for argon — it has 18 protons.

H Hydrogen 1 Proton no. = 1	**He** Helium 2 Proton no. = 2

Li Lithium 2,1 Proton no. = 3	**Be** Beryllium 2,2 Proton no. = 4	**B** Boron 2,3 Proton no. = 5	**C** Carbon 2,4 Proton no. = 6	**N** Nitrogen 2,5 Proton no. = 7	**O** Oxygen 2,6 Proton no. = 8	**F** Fluorine 2,7 Proton no. = 9	**Ne** Neon 2,8 Proton no. = 10
Na Sodium 2,8,1 Proton no. = 11	**Mg** Magnesium 2,8,2 Proton no. = 12	**Al** Aluminium 2,8,3 Proton no. = 13	**Si** Silicon 2,8,4 Proton no. = 14	**P** Phosphorus 2,8,5 Proton no. = 15	**S** Sulfur 2,8,6 Proton no. = 16	**Cl** Chlorine 2,8,7 Proton no. = 17	**Ar** Argon 2,8,8 Proton no. = 18

K Potassium 2,8,8,1 Proton no. = 19	**Ca** Calcium 2,8,8,2 Proton no. = 20

Answer... To calculate the electronic structure of argon, follow the rules. It's got 18 protons, so it must have 18 electrons. The first shell must have 2 electrons, the second shell must have 8, and so the third shell must have 8 as well. It's as easy as 2, 8, 8.

One little duck and two fat ladies — 2, 8, 8...

You need to know enough about electron shells to draw out that whole diagram at the bottom of the page without looking at it. The best thing to do is to just learn the pattern — don't learn each element separately.

Elements and Numbers

This page is full of useful facts about <u>elements</u> and the funny <u>numbers</u> that tell you their life story...

Elements <u>Contain One Type</u> of <u>Atom Only</u>

Quite a lot of everyday substances are <u>elements</u>:

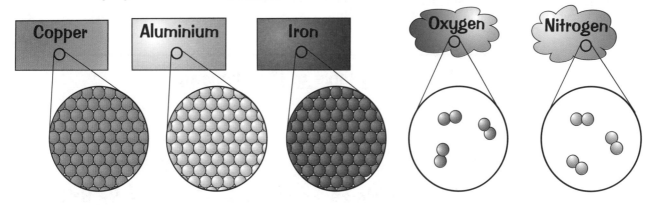

<u>Each Element</u> has an <u>Atomic Number</u> and a <u>Mass Number</u>

1) The <u>atomic number</u> says how many <u>protons</u> there are in an atom.

2) The <u>atomic number</u> of each element is <u>different</u>.

3) This is because <u>each element</u> has a <u>certain number</u> of protons.

4) It's the <u>number of protons</u> in an atom that decides what element it is.

5) For example, any atom of the element <u>helium</u> will have <u>2 protons</u>. Any atom with <u>2 protons</u> will be a <u>helium</u> atom.

6) The <u>mass number</u> is the total number of <u>protons and neutrons</u> in the atom.

Example: Oxygen

<u>The Mass Number</u>
— Total number of protons and neutrons

16

O

<u>The Atomic Number</u>
— Number of protons

8

<u>Relative Atomic Mass</u> <u>is an Average</u>

1) Sometimes there are <u>different forms</u> of the <u>same element</u>.

2) These forms have the <u>same number of protons</u> but a <u>different number of neutrons</u>.

3) This means each form has a <u>different mass number</u>.

4) You can use <u>all</u> the different mass numbers to work out the <u>average</u> mass.

5) The <u>average mass</u> of the <u>different forms</u> of an element is known as its <u>relative atomic mass</u>.

The average mass is worked out by adding up all the different mass numbers and then dividing by the number of forms.

Mass number 1 — 4:00 am daily in the monastery chapel...

It's a pretty good idea to make sure you know the <u>mass number</u> of an element from the <u>atomic number</u>.

A Brief History of the Periodic Table

In the 1800s chemists wanted to find <u>patterns</u> in the elements they knew about.

Mendeleev Put the Elements in Groups

1) In <u>1869</u>, a scientist called <u>Mendeleev</u> put all the elements he knew about in a <u>table</u> (see below).

Mendeleev's Table of the Elements

H																	
Li	Be											B	C	N	O	F	
Na	Mg											Al	Si	P	S	Cl	
K	Ca	*	Ti	V	Cr	Mn	Fe	Co	Ni	Cu	Zn	*	*	As	Se	Br	
Rb	Sr	Y	Zr	Nb	Mo	*	Ru	Rh	Pd	Ag	Cd	In	Sn	Sb	Te	I	
Cs	Ba	*	*	Ta	W	*	Os	Ir	Pt	Au	Hg	Tl	Pb	Bi			

2) He did this based on their <u>properties</u> and the properties of their <u>compounds</u>.

3) Mendeleev's table placed elements with <u>similar properties</u> in the same <u>vertical groups</u> (columns).

4) Mendeleev found that he had to leave <u>gaps</u> in his table to make this work.

The properties of an element are what it's like and how it reacts.

Mendeleev Used His Table to Predict New Elements

1) The <u>gaps</u> in Mendeleev's table of elements were really clever.

2) Mendeleev used the gaps to <u>predict</u> the properties of <u>elements</u> that hadn't been discovered yet.

3) <u>New elements</u> (e.g. scandium) have now been found which <u>fit into the gaps</u> left in Mendeleev's table.

4) Mendeleev's table has been <u>improved</u> and is now the <u>periodic table</u> we use today (see <u>next page</u> for more on this)...

A table with holes in it — not as useless as it sounds...

This shows that an <u>observation</u> (see p.1, e.g. "elements can be grouped in a table using their properties") can be used to <u>make predictions</u> (e.g. "there are gaps so there must be some undiscovered elements to fill those gaps").

The Periodic Table

The modern periodic table is a better version of Mendeleev's Table of Elements (see previous page).

Metals and Non-metals are on Opposite Sides of the Periodic Table

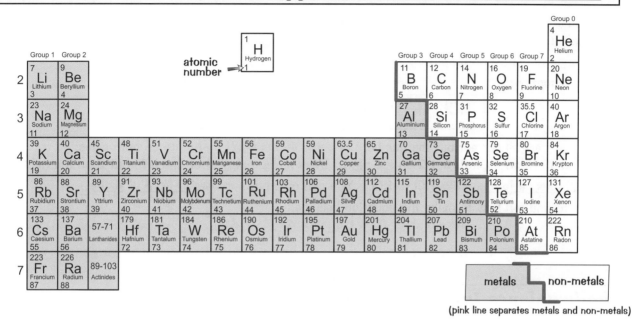

(pink line separates metals and non-metals)

The Periodic Table is Arranged in Periods and Groups

Periods

1) The rows of the periodic table are called periods.

2) The elements are arranged in order of increasing atomic number along each row.

3) E.g. the atomic numbers of the Period 2 elements increase from 3 for Li (lithium) to 10 for Ne (neon).

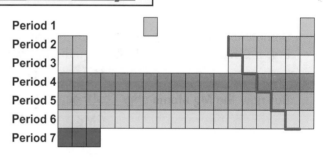

Groups

1) The columns of the periodic table are called groups.

2) Elements in the same group have similar properties.

3) This is because they have the same number of electrons in their outer shell (learn this).

4) The group number is the same as the number of outer shell electrons (except for Group 0 — they have 8 electrons in their outer shell, not 0).

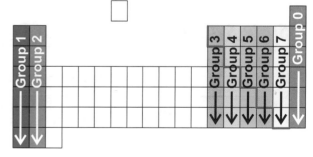

Do a bit of group work and learn this page...

You can tell if an element is a metal or a non-metal just by looking at the periodic table. Clever.

C2a Topic 1 — Atomic Structure and the Periodic Table

Balancing Equations

Equations need a lot of practice if you're going to get them right.

Balancing the Equation — Match Them Up One by One

1) There must always be the <u>same</u> number of atoms of each element on <u>both sides</u> — they can't just <u>disappear</u>.

2) You <u>balance</u> the equation by putting numbers <u>in front</u> of the <u>formulas</u> where needed.

3) Take this equation:

$$HCl \ + \ CuO \ \rightarrow \ CuCl_2 \ + \ H_2O$$

4) The <u>formulas</u> are all correct but the numbers of some atoms <u>don't match up</u> on both sides. There's only 1 Cl on the left, but 2 on the right. There's also only 1 H on the left, but 2 on the right.

5) You <u>can't change formulas</u> like HCl to HCl_2. You can only put numbers <u>in front of them</u>.

6) Read on to find out how to make the equation balance...

Method: Balance Just ONE Type of Atom at a Time

In the equation above you're <u>short of Cl atoms on the left</u>.
The <u>only</u> thing you can do about that is make it 2HCl instead of just HCl:

$$2HCl \ + \ CuO \ \rightarrow \ CuCl_2 \ + \ H_2O$$

<u>Everything balances</u>. The hydrogen atoms didn't balance before but now they've <u>sorted themselves out</u>.

Remember, don't change the little numbers. Only change the big numbers in front of the formulas.

Sometimes making <u>one type</u> of atom balance will <u>unbalance</u> some of the others.
E.g. a 2 has been added to this equation to <u>balance</u> the O atoms:

$$Mg \ + \ O_2 \ \rightarrow \ 2MgO$$

But now the Mg atoms <u>aren't balanced</u>. So, a <u>new number</u> is added to balance them:

$$2Mg \ + \ O_2 \ \rightarrow \ 2MgO$$

State Symbols Tell You What Physical State a Chemical Is In

1) The physical state of a chemical is whether it's a <u>solid</u>, <u>liquid</u>, <u>gas</u> or <u>dissolved</u> in water.

2) <u>State symbols</u> show the state a chemical is in. These are easy enough, <u>so make sure you know them</u>.

| (s) — Solid | (l) — Liquid | (g) — Gas | (aq) — Aqueous (dissolved in water) |

E.g. $\quad\quad\quad 2Mg_{(s)} \ + \ O_{2(g)} \ \rightarrow \ 2MgO_{(s)}$

Balancing equations — weigh it up in your mind...

A number in <u>front</u> of a formula affects the <u>whole formula</u>. So, $\underline{3}Na_2SO_4$ means 3 lots of Na_2SO_4.
The little numbers in the <u>middle</u> or at the <u>end</u> of a formula <u>only</u> apply to the atom <u>right before</u>.
So the 4 in Na_2SO_4 just means 4 Os, not 4 Ss. The 2 just means 2 Na atoms.

Ionic Bonding

Atoms of different elements can form <u>chemical bonds</u> and join together to create <u>new compounds</u>.

Ionic Bonding — Transferring Electrons

1) In <u>ionic bonding</u>, atoms <u>lose or gain electrons</u> to form <u>ions</u>.
2) An ion is an <u>atom</u> (or group of atoms) with a + or − <u>charge</u>.
3) <u>Oppositely</u> charged ions are <u>attracted</u> to each other to form <u>ionic bonds</u>.

A Shell with Just One or Two Electrons Wants to Lose Them...

1) Atoms with just <u>one or two electrons</u> in their outer shell want to <u>lose</u> these.
2) They will then be <u>positive</u> ions with a <u>full shell</u>.

A Nearly Full Shell Wants to Gain Electrons...

1) Atoms with <u>nearly full</u> outer shells want to <u>gain</u> an <u>extra one or two electrons</u>.
2) So they <u>take</u> an electron (or two) from an atom that wants to lose one (or two).
3) This turns them into <u>negative</u> ions with a <u>full shell</u>.
4) The positive and negative ions are then <u>attracted</u> to each other.
   For example, sodium and chlorine react to make <u>sodium chloride</u>:

The <u>sodium</u> (Na) atom <u>loses</u> its <u>outer</u> electron and becomes an Na⁺ ion.

The <u>chlorine</u> (Cl) atom has <u>picked up</u> the <u>spare electron</u> and becomes a Cl⁻ ion.

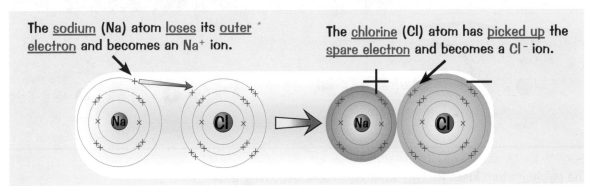

Groups 1 & 2 and 6 & 7 are the Most Likely to Form Ions

1) Groups 1, 2, 6 and 7 elements form <u>ions</u> easily.
2) <u>Group 1 and 2</u> elements <u>lose</u> their outer shell electrons to form <u>+ve ions</u> (<u>cations</u>).
3) <u>Group 6 and 7</u> elements <u>gain</u> their outer shell electrons to form <u>−ve ions</u> (<u>anions</u>).

Cations		Anions	
Group 1	Group 2	Group 6	Group 7
Li^+	Be^{2+}	O^{2-}	F^-
Na^+	Mg^{2+}		Cl^-
K^+	Ca^{2+}		

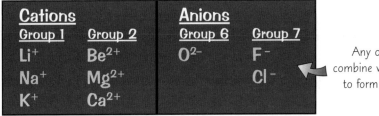

Any of these anions can combine with any of the cations to form an ionic compound.

Any old ion, any old ion — any, any, any old ion...

Remember, the + and − charges only appear when an atom <u>reacts</u> with something and becomes an ion.

Ionic Compounds

Make sure you've really got your head around the idea of ionic bonding before you start on this page.

Ionic Compounds All Form in a Similar Way

These diagrams show what happens to the electrons in ionic bonds:

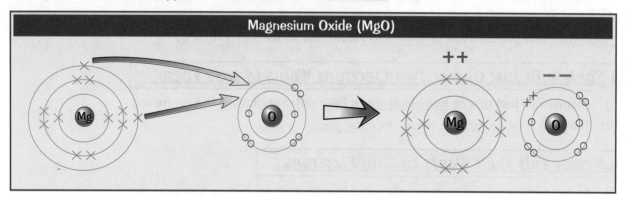

Magnesium Oxide (MgO)

- The magnesium atom loses its two outer electrons, becoming an Mg^{2+} Ion.
- The oxygen atom picks up the two electrons, becoming an O^{2-} (oxide) ion.

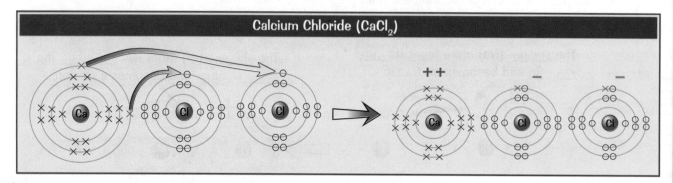

Calcium Chloride (CaCl$_2$)

- The calcium atom loses its two outer electrons, becoming a Ca^{2+} ion.
- The two chlorine atoms pick up one electron each, becoming two Cl$^-$ (chloride) ions.

> The atoms end up with full outer shells after giving and taking electrons.

Ionic Compounds Have Similar Properties

1) Ionic compounds have high melting points and high boiling points.
2) They don't conduct electricity when solid.
3) But, they do conduct electricity when in aqueous solution (dissolved in water) or molten (melted).

Full shells — it's the name of the game...

It takes lots of heat to melt ionic compounds. But after that they get all excited and start conducting electricity.

Naming Compounds and Finding Formulas

In chemistry it's not just a chemical's name you need to get right, it's the formula too.

Naming Compounds — Two Simple Rules

RULE 1: When two different elements join together the compound's name is 'something -IDE'.

E.g.
- If sodium and chlorine join together, you get a compound called sodium chloride.
- If magnesium and oxygen join together, you get a compound called magnesium oxide.

RULE 2: When three or more different elements join together and one of them is oxygen, the compound's name is 'something -ATE'.

E.g.
- Copper, sulfur and oxygen join together to make copper sulfate.
- Sodium, nitrogen and oxygen join together to make sodium nitrate.

Look at Charges to Work Out the Formula of an Ionic Compound

To work out what formula you get when things react, you can look at what ions they form.

Positive Ions (Cations)		Negative Ions (Anions)	
1^+ ions	2^+ ions	2^- ions	1^- ions
All Group 1 metals, including:	All Group 2 metals, including:	Carbonate CO_3^{2-}	Hydroxide OH^-
Lithium Li^+	Magnesium Mg^{2+}	Sulfate SO_4^{2-}	Nitrate NO_3^-
Sodium Na^+	Calcium Ca^{2+}	All Group 6 elements, including:	All Group 7 elements, including:
Potassium K^+		Oxide O^{2-}	Fluoride F^-
		Sulfide S^{2-}	Chloride Cl^-
			Bromide Br^-
			Iodide I^-

The charges of the ions in a compound have to balance. For example...

Sodium hydroxide

1) You need 1 hydroxide ion (OH^-) to balance the charge of 1 sodium ion (Na^+). This means that a 1+ charge balances a 1- charge.

2) So the formula for sodium hydroxide would be NaOH.

Magnesium chloride

1) You need 2 chloride ions (Cl^-) to balance the charge of 1 magnesium ion (Mg^{2+}). This means that a 2+ charge balances two 1- charges.

2) So the formula for magnesium chloride would be $MgCl_2$.

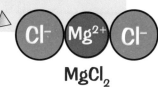

$MgCl_2$

Me sulfate — you sulfide...

Compounds are neutral (they don't have an overall charge) so all the charges in them must balance out to zero.

Preparing Insoluble Salts

Some salts are <u>soluble</u> (they dissolve) and some are <u>insoluble</u> (they don't dissolve).

The Rules

You need to learn whether these substances are soluble or not:

Substance	Soluble or Insoluble?
salts of sodium, potassium and ammonium	soluble
nitrates	soluble
chlorides	soluble (except silver chloride and lead chloride)
sulfates	soluble (except lead, barium and calcium sulfate)
carbonates and hydroxides	insoluble (except for sodium, potassium and ammonium ones)

Making Insoluble Salts — Precipitation Reactions

This is when the product of the reaction is a precipitate (solid).

1) To make a pure, dry sample of an <u>insoluble</u> salt, you can use a <u>precipitation reaction</u>.

2) You just need to pick the right two <u>soluble salts</u>, they <u>react</u> and you get your <u>insoluble salt</u>.

3) E.g. to make <u>lead chloride</u> (insoluble), mix <u>lead nitrate</u> and <u>sodium chloride</u> (both soluble).

lead nitrate + sodium chloride → lead chloride + sodium nitrate

Method

Stage 1

1) In a test tube dissolve some <u>lead nitrate</u> in <u>distilled water</u>.
2) In another test tube dissolve some <u>sodium chloride</u> in distilled water.
3) Tip the <u>two solutions</u> into a beaker and <u>stir well</u>.
4) The lead chloride should <u>precipitate</u> out.

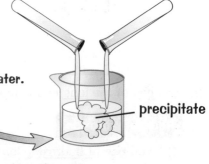

precipitate

filter paper

filter funnel

Stage 2

1) Put a folded piece of <u>filter paper</u> into a <u>filter funnel</u>.
2) Use it to <u>filter</u> the contents of the beaker into a <u>flask</u>.

Stage 3

1) Rinse the solid with distilled water to make sure that <u>all the soluble sodium nitrate</u> has been washed away.
2) Scrape the <u>lead chloride</u> onto clean filter paper and leave to dry.

Soluble or insoluble? That is the question...

In the exam, you might have to use the <u>rules</u> to predict whether a <u>precipitate</u> will be formed when two solutions are mixed together. If it is, you might have to <u>name</u> it. Be prepared and you'll be fine.

Barium Meals and Flame Tests

This page is a bit of a mish mash. It's about drinking <u>barium sulfate</u> (eurghh) but it's also about pretty <u>coloured flames</u> (ooo... ahh). It all needs learning though.

Barium Sulfate _Can Be Used for_ X-Rays

<u>Barium sulfate</u> is pretty useful...

1) Normally only <u>bones</u> show up when you have an <u>X-ray</u>.

2) But, barium sulfate is <u>opaque</u> to <u>X-rays</u> (they can't pass through it).

3) When <u>drunk</u> it shows up the <u>gut</u> in an X-ray picture.
   This means any <u>problems</u> (e.g. blockages) can be seen.

4) Most barium salts are <u>toxic</u>. But barium sulfate is <u>safe to drink</u> because it's <u>insoluble</u>.
   This means it can't enter the <u>blood</u>. It just passes through the body.

5) When a patient <u>drinks</u> barium sulfate before an X-ray it's called a <u>barium meal</u>.

Flame Tests — _Spot the Colour_

1) Some metals give a <u>colourful flame</u>. You see this every November 5th when a <u>firework explodes</u>. So, remember, remember...

<u>Sodium</u> ions (Na^+) give a yellow/orange flame.

<u>Potassium</u> ions (K^+) give a lilac flame.

<u>Calcium</u> ions (Ca^{2+}) give a brick-red flame.

<u>Copper</u> ions (Cu^{2+}) give a blue-green flame.

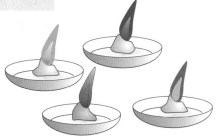

2) So if you stick a bit of <u>copper wire</u> in a Bunsen flame, you'll see a <u>blue-green flame</u>.

3) Flame tests don't just work when you've got a sample of a <u>pure element</u>.
   They also work with a <u>compound</u> that contains that element.

4) So if you stick a sample of <u>copper sulfate</u> in a Bunsen flame,
   you'll also see a <u>blue-green flame</u> because of the Cu^{2+} <u>ions</u>.

Testing metals is flaming useful...

Make sure you learn both halves of this page, don't just skip down to the cool <u>fireworks</u> bit.

Testing for Negative Ions and Spectroscopy

So you've learnt about flame tests on the page before this, but there are more ways you can test for ions.

Testing for Carbonate Ions, CO_3^{2-} — Check for CO_2

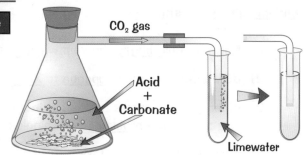

1) Carbonates react with <u>dilute acids</u> to form <u>carbon dioxide</u>.

> acid + carbonate → salt + water + carbon dioxide

2) So, you can react a sample with <u>dilute acid</u>. If carbon dioxide forms then <u>carbonate</u> ions (CO_3^{2-}) must have been present.

3) You can test for <u>carbon dioxide</u> by bubbling a gas through <u>limewater</u>. If the gas is <u>carbon dioxide</u>, the <u>limewater turns milky</u>.

Test for Sulfates and Chlorides

Sulfate Ions, SO_4^{2-}

1) To test for a <u>sulfate</u> ion (SO_4^{2-}) in a solution, <u>add dilute hydrochloric acid</u> (HCl). Then add <u>barium chloride solution</u>, $BaCl_2$.

2) If <u>sulfate</u> ions are present you get a <u>white</u> precipitate of <u>barium sulfate</u>.

$$Ba^{2+}(aq) + SO_4^{2-}(aq) \longrightarrow BaSO_4(s)$$

Chloride Ions, Cl^-

1) To test for <u>chloride</u> ions (Cl^-) in a solution, add <u>dilute nitric acid</u> (HNO_3). Then add <u>silver nitrate solution</u> ($AgNO_3$).

2) If <u>chloride</u> ions are present you get a <u>white</u> precipitate of <u>silver chloride</u>.

$$Ag^+(aq) + Cl^-(aq) \longrightarrow AgCl(s)$$

Spectroscopy Can Be Used to Identify Elements

beep beep... vrrrr... definitely sodium

1) Elements in a sample can be <u>identified</u> using <u>spectroscopy</u>. It's a little bit like a flame test (see previous page) — it uses colours to identify elements.

2) Spectroscopy can detect even very <u>small amounts</u> of elements in a sample.

3) Spectroscopy has also allowed scientists to discover <u>new elements</u>. For example, <u>rubidium</u> and <u>caesium</u> were both discovered using spectroscopy.

Just let me get my spectracles on to identify this ion...

You need to know the tests for <u>carbonate</u>, <u>sulfate</u> and <u>chloride</u> ions. Cover the page and scribble them down.

Covalent Bonding

Not all atoms form ionic bonds (see page 49). Luckily, there's another option — covalent bonding...

Covalent Bonds — Sharing Electrons

1) Atoms can make covalent bonds by sharing a pair of electrons between two atoms.
2) This way both atoms feel that they have a full outer shell.
3) Each atom has to make enough covalent bonds to fill up its outer shell.
4) When atoms make covalent bonds with one or more other atoms, they form a molecule.
5) Learn these four important examples:

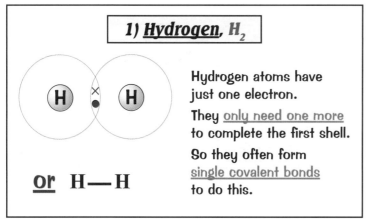

1) Hydrogen, H_2

Hydrogen atoms have just one electron.

They only need one more to complete the first shell.

So they often form single covalent bonds to do this.

or H—H

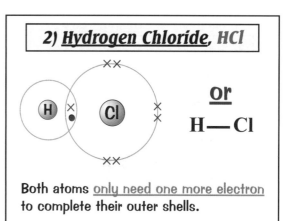

2) Hydrogen Chloride, HCl

or H—Cl

Both atoms only need one more electron to complete their outer shells.

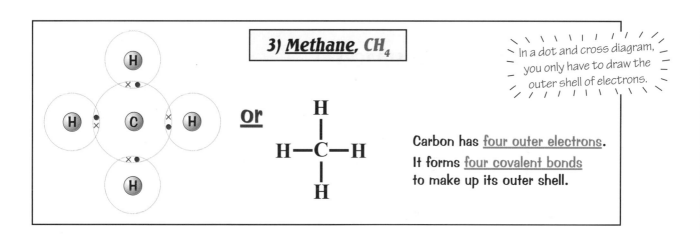

3) Methane, CH_4

or

H
|
H—C—H
|
H

Carbon has four outer electrons. It forms four covalent bonds to make up its outer shell.

> In a dot and cross diagram, you only have to draw the outer shell of electrons.

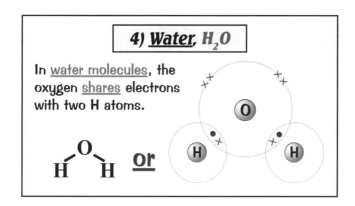

4) Water, H_2O

In water molecules, the oxygen shares electrons with two H atoms.

or

> Fancy sharing spare electrons?

Covalent bonding — it's good to share...

Make sure you learn these four really basic examples and why they work. Every atom wants a full outer shell, and they can get that either by becoming an ion (see page 49) or by sharing electrons.

Covalent Substances — Two Kinds

There are two kinds of covalent substance: <u>simple molecular</u> and <u>giant molecular</u>.

Simple Molecular Covalent Substances

1) Simple molecular substances are made up of <u>small molecules</u> with <u>strong</u> covalent bonds.

2) The molecules have <u>weak forces between them</u> so they are <u>easily parted</u> from each other.

3) This means that the <u>melting points</u> and <u>boiling points</u> are <u>very low</u>.

4) Molecular substances <u>don't conduct electricity</u> — simply because there are <u>no ions</u>.

Very weak forces between molecules

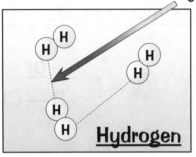 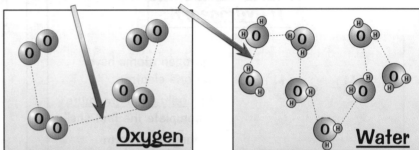

Giant Molecular Covalent Substances

1) In giant covalent structures, <u>all</u> the atoms are <u>bonded</u> to <u>each other</u> by <u>strong</u> covalent bonds.

2) The <u>main examples</u> are <u>diamond</u> and <u>graphite</u>, which are both made only from <u>carbon atoms</u>.

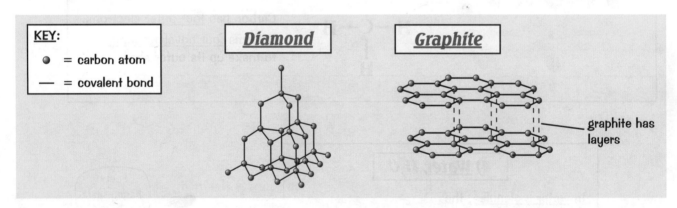

3) The strong bonds mean that giant covalent substance have <u>very high</u> melting points and <u>very high</u> boiling points.

4) Also, they <u>don't conduct electricity</u> (except for graphite).

Carbon is a girl's best friend...

The <u>two different types</u> of covalent substance are very different — make sure you know about them both.

Classifying Elements and Compounds

Put on your tweed jacket and spectacles — it's time for a bit of <u>detective work</u>...

Working Out the Bonding in a Substance by its Properties

You should be able to <u>work out</u> whether substances are:

- <u>ionic</u> (see p.50),
- <u>giant molecular</u> (see p.56), or
- <u>simple molecular</u> (see p.56).

That's the guy.

In the Exam they might describe the <u>properties</u> of a substance and ask you to decide <u>which type of structure</u> it has. Try this one:

Example: Seven substances were tested for melting point, boiling point and how well they conduct electricity. Here are the results:

Some of the substances don't have melting or boiling points. This is because the molecules decompose (break up) instead. E.g. if something decomposes before it boils, then it won't have a boiling point.

Substance	Melting point (°C)	Boiling point (°C)	Good electrical conductor when solid?	Good electrical conductor when in solution?
sodium chloride	801	1413	no	yes
magnesium sulfate	1124	decomposes	no	yes
hexane	−95	69	no	no (insoluble)
liquid paraffin	4	224	no	no (insoluble)
silicon(IV) oxide	1650	2230	no	no (insoluble)
copper sulfate	decomposes	none — already decomposed	no	yes
sucrose (sugar)	186	decomposes	no	soluble but doesn't conduct

Work out the type of bonding in each substance.

Answer:

- <u>Sodium chloride</u>, <u>magnesium sulfate</u> and <u>copper sulfate</u> all <u>conduct</u> electricity when <u>dissolved</u>, but not when solid. So, they must be <u>ionic substances</u>.

- <u>Hexane</u> and <u>liquid paraffin don't conduct</u> electricity at all. They have <u>low</u> melting and boiling points. So, they must be <u>simple molecular</u> covalent substances.

- <u>Silicon(IV) oxide doesn't conduct</u> electricity. It has <u>high</u> melting and boiling points. So, it must be a <u>giant molecular</u> substance.

- <u>Sucrose</u> doesn't conduct electricity even in solution so it <u>can't be an ionic substance</u>. It has a <u>low</u> melting point. So, it must be a <u>simple molecular</u> substance.

Simple molecules? — not so sure about that...

If you're stuck trying to work out the answer, decide what it definitely <u>can't</u> be and see what you're left with.

Separation Techniques

There are different ways of <u>separating</u> mixtures of liquids. It depends how easily the liquids mix together...

Miscible Liquids Mix Together but Immiscible Liquids Don't

1) Some liquids will <u>mix</u> with each other — and some <u>won't</u>.

2) Liquids that <u>mix together</u> form <u>miscible</u> mixtures. For example, milk mixes with tea.

3) Liquids that <u>don't mix together properly</u> form <u>immiscible</u> mixtures.
   For example, oil doesn't mix with water — it just floats on the top.

Use a Separating Funnel to Separate Immiscible Liquids

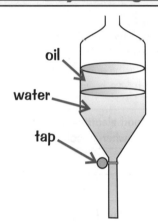

oil

water

tap

1) <u>Shake</u> two <u>immiscible</u> liquids together.

2) Let them <u>stand</u> so they <u>separate</u> out into layers.

3) Use a <u>separating funnel</u> with a <u>tap</u> to separate these layers.

4) The tap can be opened to <u>drain</u> off the lower layer into a beaker.

Fractional Distillation Separates Out Miscible Liquids

1) Mixtures of <u>miscible liquids</u> can be separated by <u>fractional distillation</u>.

2) The mixture is <u>heated</u> so that the liquids become gases.
   The gases rise up the column and <u>cool down</u>.

3) When the gases cool down enough they will <u>condense</u>.

Condense means to turn from a gas into a liquid.

4) But the different liquids will <u>condense at different temperatures</u>.
   They can then be collected <u>separately</u>.

5) We can <u>fractionally distil liquid air</u>.
   The products include nitrogen and oxygen.

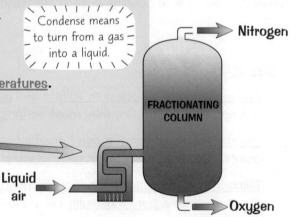

Nitrogen

FRACTIONATING
COLUMN

Liquid
air

Oxygen

Exams + fun = immiscible...

So, there's two techniques used to separate mixtures of liquids — <u>funnels</u> for <u>immiscible</u> liquids and <u>fractional</u> <u>distillation</u> for <u>miscible</u> liquids. Don't be put off by the weird words for liquids that don't mix and liquids that do.

Chromatography

Paper chromatography is pretty clever. You need to know how to do it and how to use the results.

Chromatography Can Be Used to Identify Substances

Here's how to use paper chromatography to identify substances in a sample:

1) Draw a line in pencil near the bottom of some filter paper.

2) Put spots of each sample being tested on it.

3) Roll up the paper and put it in a beaker containing a solvent (a liquid such as ethanol or water).

4) The solvent soaks up the paper, taking the samples with it.

5) The different substances in the sample travel up the paper at different speeds. So they form spots in different places.

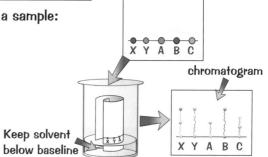

Keep solvent below baseline

chromatogram

USING CHROMATOGRAPHY RESULTS

1) One use for chromatography is to separate out the mixture of dyes in food.

2) You can compare the results against the results from known colouring agents to identify the dyes.

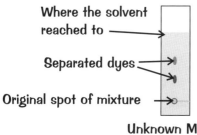

Where the solvent reached to

Separated dyes

Original spot of mixture

Unknown Mixture

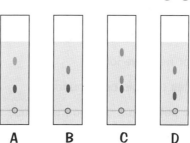

A   B   C   D

You can see that the unknown mixture is the same as mixture B.

You can Calculate the R_f Value for Each Substance

1) You need to know how to work out the R_f values for spots on a chromatogram.

2) An R_f value compares the distance travelled by the substance and the distance travelled by the solvent.

3) You can find R_f values using the formula:

$$R_f = \frac{\text{distance travelled by substance}}{\text{distance travelled by solvent}}$$

4) R_f values are used in the food industry and in forensic science.

Forensic science is science used to solve a crime.

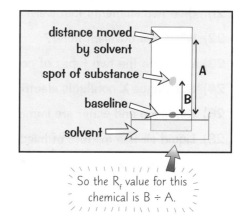

distance moved by solvent

spot of substance

baseline

solvent

A

B

So the R_f value for this chemical is B ÷ A.

5) Scientists use R_f values to identify food additives and drugs.

Comb-atography — identifies strange things in your hair...

Draw your baseline and any labels in pencil not pen — ink will dissolve in the solvent and confuse your results.

Revision Summary for C2a Topics 1, 2 & 3

Ooo, the end of the section. Well, they do say that time flies when you're having fun. Why stop now? You might as well have a go at these and find out which bits you need to read again.

1) a) Name the three types of particle in an atom.
    b) State the relative mass and charge of each particle.

2) The element boron has 5 protons. How many electrons does a boron atom have in its outer shell?

3) Potassium has 19 protons. Work out its electronic configuration.

4) Is it the number of protons or the number of neutrons that decides what element an atom is?

5) What do the mass number and atomic number represent?

6) What is relative atomic mass?

7) Explain how Mendeleev arranged known elements in a table. How did he predict new elements?

8) "Elements in the modern periodic table are in order of atomic number." True or false?

9) What are columns in the periodic table called?

10)* Balance this equation: $CaCO_3 + HCl \rightarrow CaCl_2 + H_2O + CO_2$

11) What happens to the electrons when two atoms form an ionic bond?

12) Are cations positive or negative ions?

13) List the main properties of ionic compounds.

14) Explain the difference between a compound whose name ends in '-ate' and one whose name ends in '-ide'.

15)* Work out the formulas of these ionic compounds:
    a) potassium chloride   b) calcium fluoride

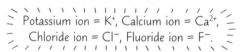
Potassium ion = K^+, Calcium ion = Ca^{2+}, Chloride ion = Cl^-, Fluoride ion = F^-.

16) Name two insoluble metal chlorides.

17) Describe how you would prepare a pure, dry sample of the insoluble salt lead sulfate using lead nitrate and sodium sulfate.

18) Explain why barium sulfate can be drunk even though it's toxic.

19) In a flame test, a metal gives a blue-green flame. Name the metal.

20) How would you test for sulfate ions in a solution?

21) Give two elements that were discovered by spectroscopy.

22) What is a covalent bond?

23) What are the two types of covalent substance?

24)*Substance X conducts electricity only when in solution. What type of bonding does Substance X have?

25) Kerosene and water are immiscible. Describe how you could separate a mixture of these two liquids.

26) Liquid air is a mixture of miscible liquids. Name the method that can be used to separate them.

27) Describe how paper chromatography could be used to identify colouring agents in food.

28)*What is the R_f value of a chemical that moves 4.5 cm when the solvent moves 12 cm?

* Answers on page 108

Properties of Metals

Metals — they're probably better than you think.

Metals are on the Left and Middle of the Periodic Table

1) Most of the elements are metals — so they cover most of the periodic table.

2) Only the elements on the far right are non-metals.

3) The transition metals are found in the centre block of the periodic table.

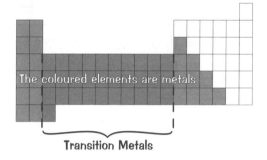

The coloured elements are metals

Transition Metals

All metals have similar properties.
1) They conduct electricity well.
2) They're malleable — this means they can be bent or hammered into different shapes.

Most metals are transition metals. They have the normal properties of metals and they also:
1) have high melting points.
2) form very colourful compounds.

It's the Structure of Metals That Gives Them Their Properties

1) Metals are made up of lots of metal atoms held together by metallic bonds.

2) The metallic bonds allow the outer electron(s) of each atom to become delocalised (move freely).

3) This means the metal is made up of a regular arrangement (pattern) of positive ions and a "sea" of delocalised (free) electrons.

4) The electrons can move freely so metals are good conductors of electricity.

5) The strong bonds give metals very high melting points and high boiling points.

6) The strong bonds also mean that metals are insoluble in water — they won't dissolve.

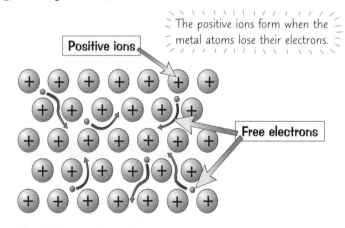

The positive ions form when the metal atoms lose their electrons.

Positive ions

Free electrons

Metals used to be found on buses — they're great conductors...

Ah, now I see why a transition metal is the material of choice for aliens or robots trying to take over the world. With a hammer and a lot of muscle you may be able to bend them but they won't break easily. And unless you have a very hot oven they won't melt either. Sounds good to me — I'm off to put on my suit of armour...

Group 1 — The Alkali Metals

If you want elements that fizz, then the <u>alkali metals</u> are the ones for you.

Alkali Metals are <u>Soft</u> and Have <u>Low Melting Points</u>

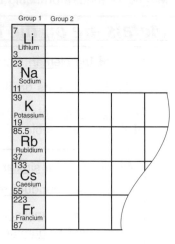

The metals in <u>Group 1</u> of the periodic table are known as the <u>alkali metals</u>.
They're different to other metals in <u>two</u> ways:

> 1) They're <u>soft</u> — they can be cut with a knife.
>
> 2) They have <u>low melting points</u> compared with other metals.

Group 1 Elements <u>React</u> <u>with</u> <u>Water</u>

1) When <u>lithium</u>, <u>sodium</u> or <u>potassium</u> are put in <u>water</u>, they react to form <u>hydroxides</u>.

2) The <u>hydroxides</u> form <u>alkaline solutions</u>. This is why Group 1 metals are known as the <u>alkali metals</u>.

3) As you move <u>down</u> Group 1, the elements get <u>more reactive</u>.

Example: The reaction between lithium and water

Water

Lithium hydroxide solution

Lithium

A lump of lithium is added to water.

The lump of lithium fizzes around on the surface.

The lithium disappears. Lithium hydroxide (an alkaline solution) is made.

4) You can see this in the time it takes the different elements to <u>react completely</u> with the water and disappear.

5) <u>Lithium</u> takes longer than sodium or potassium to react, so it's the <u>least reactive</u>. <u>Potassium</u> takes the shortest time to react of these three elements, so it's the <u>most reactive</u>.

6) You can use this to <u>predict</u> how reactive <u>other alkali metals</u> are with water. E.g. <u>sodium</u> is <u>between</u> lithium and potassium in Group 1. So, it will react <u>faster</u> with water than <u>lithium</u>, but <u>slower</u> than <u>potassium</u>.

Reaction with Water Produces <u>Hydrogen Gas</u>

1) The <u>reaction</u> of an alkali metal with water produces hydrogen — this is what you can see <u>fizzing</u>.

2) These reactions can be written down as <u>chemical equations</u> — e.g. for <u>sodium</u> the equation is...

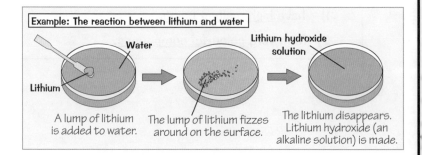

In words: sodium + water $\rightarrow$ sodium hydroxide + hydrogen

In symbols: $2Na_{(s)} + 2H_2O_{(l)} \rightarrow 2NaOH_{(aq)} + H_2{}_{(g)}$

There's a reason that ducks aren't made out of potassium...

Alkali metals are ace. Not only do they fizz madly but there's only <u>the reaction with water</u> and a couple of <u>properties</u> that you have to learn. So there's <u>no excuse</u> for not knowing everything on this page.

Group 7 — The Halogens

The halogens are found in Group 7 of the periodic table. Just like the alkali metals, they're really reactive...

Group 7 Elements are Known as the 'Halogens'

At room temperature:
- Chlorine is a green gas.
- Bromine is an orange liquid.
- Iodine is a dark grey solid.

 chlorine

 Bromine

 Iodine

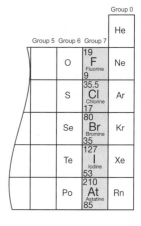

	Group 5	Group 6	Group 7	Group 0
				He
	O	S	19 F Fluorine 9	Ne
	S		35.5 Cl Chlorine 17	Ar
	Se		80 Br Bromine 35	Kr
	Te		127 I Iodine 53	Xe
	Po		210 At Astatine 85	Rn

The Halogens React with Metals to Form Metal Halides

Halogens react with most metals to form metal halides.

For example, chlorine reacts with aluminium:

aluminium + chlorine → aluminium chloride

$$2Al_{(s)} + 3Cl_{2\,(g)} \rightarrow 2AlCl_{3\,(s)}$$

Halogens Can React With Hydrogen to Form Hydrogen Halides

1) Halogens react with hydrogen to form hydrogen halides.
   For example, chlorine reacts with hydrogen to form hydrogen chloride gas.

chlorine + hydrogen → hydrogen chloride

$$Cl_{2(g)} + H_{2(g)} \rightarrow 2HCl_{(g)}$$

2) Hydrogen halides dissolve in water to form acidic solutions.

More Reactive Halogens will Displace Less Reactive Ones

1) When halides dissolve in water, the halide ions are free to react.

2) If a more reactive halogen reacts with a solution containing halide ions it will "push out" (displace) the less reactive halogen.

3) This is called a displacement reaction.

4) The higher up Group 7 an element is, the more reactive it is.

5) For example, chlorine is more reactive than iodine (it's higher up Group 7). So, chlorine reacts with potassium iodide to form potassium chloride and iodine.

A halide ion is a halogen ion, e.g. Cl⁻, Br⁻ or I⁻.

chlorine + potassium iodide → iodine + potassium chloride

$$Cl_{2\,(g)} + 2KI_{(aq)} \rightarrow I_{2(aq)} + 2KCl_{(aq)}$$

This is the equation for chlorine displacing iodine. You may be given a different example in the exam, but the equations are all quite similar.

Polish that halo and get revising...

The halogens are another group from the periodic table. Just like the alkali metals (see p.62), you've got to learn their trends and the reactions. Learn them, cover up the page, scribble, check. It's the only way it'll stick.

Group 0 — The Noble Gases

The <u>noble gases don't react</u> with very much. You can't even see them — they're a bit <u>dull</u> really.

Group 0 Elements are All Inert Gases

1) Group 0 elements are called the <u>noble gases</u>.

2) They're <u>inert</u> — this means they <u>don't react</u> with much at all.
   They have a <u>full outer shell</u> so they're <u>not</u> desperate to <u>give up</u> or <u>gain</u> electrons.

3) Noble gases are also <u>non-flammable</u> — they won't set on fire.

4) These properties mean that scientists didn't find the gases for a <u>long time</u>.

5) The gases were found when chemists noticed that the <u>density</u> of <u>nitrogen</u> made in chemical <u>reactions</u> was <u>different</u> to the density of nitrogen taken from the <u>air</u>.

6) They came up with a <u>hypothesis</u> (see page 1). They thought that the nitrogen taken from air must have <u>other gases mixed in with it</u>.

7) Scientists tested the <u>hypothesis</u> and found the different noble gases through a series of <u>experiments</u>.

Density is how heavy something is for its volume.

	Group 6	Group 7	Group 0
			4 He Helium 2
	O	F	20 Ne Neon 10
	S	Cl	40 Ar Argon 18
	Se	Br	84 Kr Krypton 36
	Te	I	131 Xe Xenon 54
	Po	At	222 Rn Radon 86

The Noble Gases have Many Everyday Uses...

1) <u>Argon</u> is used to provide an <u>inert atmosphere</u> in <u>filament lamps</u> (light bulbs). As the argon is <u>non-flammable</u> it stops the very hot filament from <u>burning away</u>.

2) Argon can also be used to protect metals that are being <u>welded</u>. The inert atmosphere stops the hot metal reacting with <u>oxygen</u>.

I love Helium

<u>Helium</u> is used in <u>airships</u> and <u>party balloons</u>. Helium has a <u>lower density</u> than air — so it makes balloons <u>float</u>.

There are Patterns in the Properties of the Noble Gases

The <u>boiling points</u> and <u>densities</u> of the noble gases <u>increase</u> as you move <u>down</u> the group. In the exam you might be asked to use this pattern to <u>predict</u> the boiling point or density of a noble gas. For example:

QUESTION

Complete the table using the numbers provided to show the boiling points of the noble gases.

Noble Gas	Boiling Point (°C)
Helium	
Neon	– 246
Argon	

-186

-269

ANSWER

1) You already know that the boiling point of the noble gases <u>increases</u> down the group.

2) This means that <u>helium</u> has a <u>lower boiling point</u> than <u>neon</u>. And <u>argon</u> has a <u>higher boiling point</u> than <u>neon</u>.

3) This tells us that the boiling point of <u>helium</u> has to be <u>−269</u> °C and the boiling point of <u>argon</u> has to be <u>−186</u> °C.

Boo! — nope, no reaction...

Well, they don't react so there's a bit less to learn about the noble gases. But, there's likely to be a question or two on them in the exam so <u>make sure you learn everything on this page</u>...

Energy Transfer in Reactions

In a chemical reaction, <u>energy</u> is always <u>taken in</u> or <u>given out</u>, and it's all about making and breaking bonds.

Energy Must Always be Supplied to Break Bonds

1) A <u>chemical reaction</u> can only happen when <u>particles</u> in the reactants <u>collide</u> (crash into each other).

2) When particles collide old bonds may be <u>broken</u> and new bonds may be <u>formed</u>.

3) Energy must be <u>used</u> to break <u>existing bonds</u> — so bond breaking is an <u>endothermic</u> process.

4) Energy is <u>released</u> (given out) when new bonds are <u>formed</u> — so bond formation is an <u>exothermic</u> process.

BOND BREAKING - <u>ENDOTHERMIC</u>

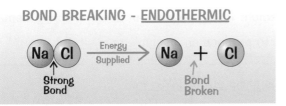

BOND FORMING - <u>EXOTHERMIC</u>

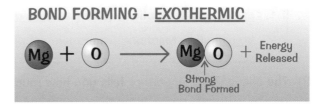

In an *Exothermic* Reaction, Energy is *Given Out*

1) In an **EXOTHERMIC** reaction, <u>more heat energy</u> is <u>given out making bonds</u> in the products than is needed to <u>break bonds</u> in the reactants.

> An <u>EXOTHERMIC reaction</u> is one which overall <u>GIVES OUT ENERGY</u> in the form of <u>heat</u>. It's shown by a <u>RISE IN TEMPERATURE</u>.

2) There are <u>two examples</u> of exothermic reactions for you to learn:
   - <u>burning fuels</u> (<u>combustion</u>).
   - <u>explosions</u>.

In an *Endothermic* Reaction, Energy is *Taken In*

1) In an <u>ENDOTHERMIC</u> reaction, <u>less heat energy</u> is <u>given out making bonds</u> in the products than is needed to <u>break bonds</u> in the reactants.

> An <u>ENDOTHERMIC reaction</u> is one which overall <u>TAKES IN ENERGY</u> in the form of <u>heat</u>. It's shown by a <u>FALL IN TEMPERATURE</u>.

2) Here are a couple of examples of endothermic reactions:
   - <u>photosynthesis</u> (the process used by plants to make food).
   - <u>ammonium nitrate dissolving</u> in water.

Right, so burning gives out heat — really...

This whole energy transfer thing is a fairly simple idea — don't be put off by the long words. Remember, "<u>exo-</u>" = <u>exit</u>, "<u>-thermic</u>" = <u>heat</u>, so an exothermic reaction is one that <u>gives out</u> heat. And "<u>endo-</u>" = erm... the other one. Okay, so there's no easy way to remember that one. Sorry.

Energy Changes and Measuring Temperature

This is about <u>measuring</u> the stuff that you learned about on the previous page.

Temperature Change <u>can be</u> Measured

1) In your exam you may be asked how you would <u>measure</u> the temperature <u>changes</u> during any of these four reactions:

> • <u>dissolving salts</u> in water.
>
> • <u>neutralisation</u> reactions (where an <u>acid</u> and <u>base</u> react together).
>
> • <u>displacement</u> reactions (where a <u>more reactive</u> element takes the place of a <u>less reactive</u> element).
>
> • <u>precipitation</u> reactions (where <u>two solutions</u> react to produce an <u>insoluble precipitate</u>).

2) The <u>change</u> in <u>temperature</u> tells you how much energy is <u>given out</u> or <u>taken in</u>.

3) You can measure the temperature change during a <u>chemical reaction</u> in solution by:

   • taking the <u>temperature of the reactants</u> at the start of the reaction,

   • <u>mixing</u> them in a <u>polystyrene cup</u>,

   • measuring the <u>temperature of the solution</u> at set points during the reaction. Easy.

4) The biggest <u>problem</u> with temperature measurements is the amount of heat <u>lost to the surroundings</u>.

5) You can reduce it a bit by putting the polystyrene cup into a <u>beaker of cotton wool</u> and putting a <u>lid</u> on the cup. This helps to keep the heat in.

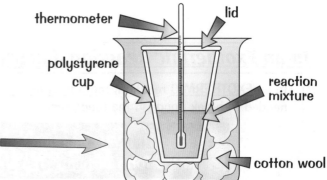

thermometer — lid

polystyrene cup

reaction mixture

cotton wool

Example — <u>Neutralising Hydrochloric Acid</u> <u>with</u> <u>Sodium Hydroxide</u>

1) Measure 25 cm³ of dilute <u>hydrochloric acid</u> using a <u>measuring cylinder</u> and put it in a <u>polystyrene cup</u>.

2) Use a <u>thermometer</u> to measure the <u>temperature</u> of the acid.

3) Place the polystyrene cup into the <u>beaker</u> containing the <u>cotton wool</u>.

4) Put 25 cm³ of dilute <u>sodium hydroxide</u> in a measuring cylinder and measure its temperature.

5) Make sure they're the <u>same temperature</u> then add the alkali to the acid. Give it a stir. Put the <u>lid</u> on the polystyrene cup.

6) Take the temperature of the mixture <u>every 30 seconds</u> and <u>record your results</u> in a table.

7) When the temperature begins to <u>fall</u>, the reaction has <u>finished</u>.

8) Work out the <u>temperature change</u> by subtracting the temperature of the acid and alkali at the <u>start</u> from the <u>highest temperature</u> recorded.

Save energy — break fewer bonds...

You can get <u>cooling packs</u> that use an <u>endothermic</u> reaction to draw heat from an injury. The pack contains two sections with different chemicals in. When you use it, you snap the middle bit and the chemicals <u>mix</u> and <u>react</u>, taking in <u>heat</u> — pretty cool, I reckon.

Rates of Reaction

Chemical reactions <u>aren't</u> all the same. There are <u>slow</u> ones (like a statue being worn down by acid rain) and <u>quick</u> ones (like a whopping great explosion). The <u>rate of reaction</u> tells you how quick a reaction will be...

Reactions Can Go at All Sorts of Different Rates

1) The <u>rate of a reaction</u> is the <u>speed</u> at which a chemical reaction takes place.

2) Reactions can be <u>very fast</u>, <u>very slow</u> or somewhere <u>in between</u>.

3) The rate of a chemical reaction depends on <u>four</u> things:

> 1) <u>Temperature</u>
> 2) <u>Concentration</u>
> 3) <u>Catalyst</u>
> 4) <u>Surface area of a solid</u>

Typical Graphs for Rate of Reaction

1) The graph below shows how the speed of a reaction changes under <u>different conditions</u>.

2) When the line becomes <u>flat</u>, the reaction has <u>ended</u> — <u>no more</u> product is being made.

3) This means that the quickest reaction is shown by the line that becomes <u>flat</u> in the <u>least</u> time.

4) The <u>quickest</u> reaction starts with the <u>steepest slope</u>, and the <u>slowest</u> reaction with the <u>shallowest slope</u>.

- <u>Graph 1</u> is a <u>fairly slow</u> reaction. The graph isn't very steep and takes a <u>long time</u> to level off.
- <u>Graphs 2 and 3</u> show the reaction taking place at a <u>faster rate</u>. The slope of the graphs gets steeper.
- <u>Graphs 1, 2 and 3</u> all meet at the same level. This shows that they all make the same amount of product. But they take <u>different</u> amounts of time to get there.

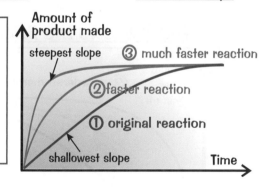

The <u>increased rate</u> could be due to <u>any</u> of these:

> a) increase in <u>temperature</u>.
> b) increase in <u>concentration</u>.
> c) <u>catalyst</u> added.
> d) an increase in <u>surface area</u> (e.g. a solid reactant crushed up into smaller bits).

Flowers and chocolates — always increase the rate of a reaction...

<u>Industrial</u> reactions usually use a <u>catalyst</u> and are done at <u>high temperature and pressure</u>. Time is money, so the faster an industrial reaction goes the better... but only <u>up to a point</u>. Chemical plants cost quite a bit to rebuild if they get blown into lots and lots of teeny tiny pieces.

Rates of Reaction Experiments

Any reaction can be used to test how the four factors affect the reaction rate (see previous page).
A really handy one for you to learn is the reaction of marble chips with hydrochloric acid.

Reaction of Hydrochloric Acid and Marble Chips

Hydrochloric acid (HCl) reacts with marble chips to produce carbon dioxide gas.

Here's how you'd use this reaction to show the effect of increasing the surface area of a solid:

1) Put the marble chips in the hydrochloric acid. Measure the volume of carbon dioxide gas given off using a gas syringe. Take readings at set times (e.g. every 15 seconds).

2) Make a table of readings. Then plot a graph with time on the x-axis and volume on the y-axis.

3) Then, repeat the experiment with the marble more crunched up (so it has a bigger surface area).

4) Then repeat with the same mass of powdered marble instead of marble chips.

5) Each time you repeat the experiment the other factors need to be kept the same. So, make sure you use exactly the same volume of acid, and exactly the same mass of marble chips.

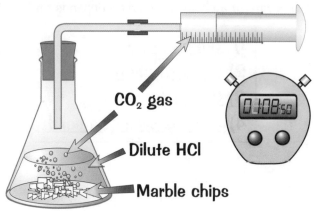

CO₂ gas

Dilute HCl

Marble chips

You can also use this reaction to test the effect of concentration and temperature on the rate of reaction (see the next page).

This Graph Shows the Effect of Increasing the Surface Area

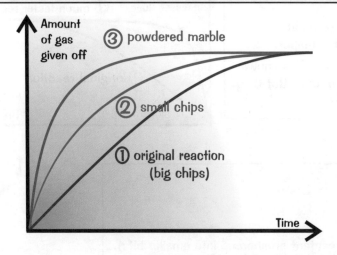

Amount of gas given off

③ powdered marble

② small chips

① original reaction (big chips)

Time

1) The powdered marble (line 3) reacted faster than the small marble chips (line 2) and the big marble chips (line 1).

2) This is because the powdered marble has the biggest surface area.

3) This shows you that an increase in surface area increases the rate of the reaction.

I'll have a large marble chips with a sprinkling of HCl please...

When you increase the surface area, there's a larger area for particles to react with. So, an increase in surface area is great for making a reaction go quicker. Ah, but what about the effect of temperature and concentration on the rate of reaction, I'm sure you're asking. Well, take a look at the next page and all should become clear...

Rates of Reaction Experiments

Ah, it's the old <u>marble chips and acid reaction</u> from the last page back again. If you aren't feeling too clear about how it works then flick back and go through it again <u>before</u> you get started on this page. Here, the reaction is used to see how <u>concentration</u> and <u>temperature</u> affect the rate of a reaction...

This Graph Shows the Effect of Increasing the Concentration

1) The method is the same as on the previous page, except this time you <u>repeat</u> the experiment using <u>different concentrations</u> of acid.

2) All of the <u>other factors</u> stay the <u>same</u> — including the size of the marble chips.

3) The <u>volume</u> of acid must always be kept <u>the same</u> too — only the <u>concentration</u> is increased.

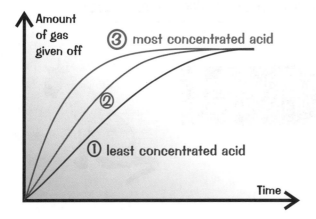

4) Plot a graph of the <u>volume of gas</u> given off as the reaction goes on.

5) The three graphs show the <u>same</u> old pattern. A <u>higher</u> concentration gives a <u>steeper graph</u> and the reaction <u>finishes</u> much quicker.

6) The <u>more</u> concentrated the acid is, the <u>faster</u> the rate of a reaction.

This Graph Shows the Effect of Increasing the Temperature

1) The <u>temperature</u> of the acid is changed by <u>warming</u> or <u>cooling</u> the flask of acid in a <u>water bath</u>.

2) All of the other factors should <u>stay the same</u>.

3) The <u>warmest acid</u> has the <u>steepest</u> curve (line 3) and the <u>coolest acid</u> has the <u>shallowest</u> curve (line 1).

4) The <u>higher</u> the temperature of the acid, the <u>faster</u> the rate of a reaction.

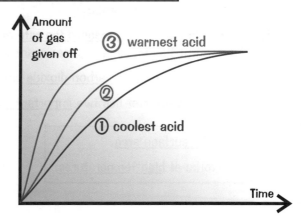

Increase your concentration — increase the mark you get on your exam...

This page should be a doddle if you know the method for the acid and marble chips reaction. You just change the <u>factor that you're looking at</u> each time and keep all of the <u>other factors the same</u>. It's pretty simple really — increasing the surface area, concentration or temperature will always <u>increase the rate</u> of a chemical reaction.

Catalysts

Catalysts are used in chemical reactions to speed things up. I wish they were used for other stuff as well though — imagine a catalyst to speed up getting out of bed in the morning...

Catalysts Speed Up the Rate of Reaction

1) Catalysts are used to speed up the rate of a reaction.

2) But catalysts aren't used up in the reaction.

3) This means a catalyst can be used over and over again.

4) Using a catalyst doesn't make more product though. The catalyst only speeds up the rate of the reaction. So the reaction will make the same amount of product but more quickly.

Learn this definition of a catalyst:

> A catalyst is a substance which changes the speed of a reaction, without being used up in the reaction.

Catalytic Converters are Used in Car Exhausts

1) Catalysts are used in catalytic converters.

2) A catalytic converter is found in a car's exhaust.

3) Car exhausts can give off poisonous gases like carbon monoxide if petrol doesn't burn properly.

4) A catalytic converter increases the rate at which carbon monoxide and unburnt fuel in exhaust gases react with oxygen in the air.

5) This reaction produces carbon dioxide and water — which aren't poisonous to humans.

6) A catalytic converter has two important features which speed up the rate of the reaction:

- large surface area.
- works at high temperatures.

Catalyst — Garfield, Sylvester, Puss in Boots, Top Cat, Bagpuss, Cat Deeley...

Pretty useful things these catalysts. They speed up loads of useful reactions. But they don't get used up themselves at the end of a reaction. So they can be used over and over again. Sadly, in some reactions it costs too much to use a catalyst, and in other reactions chemists can't find one that works. That's life I'm afraid.

Relative Formula Mass

Relative atomic mass and relative formula mass sound horrible. But they're not that bad.
Take a few deep breaths, and relax, as everything becomes clear...

Relative Atomic Mass, A_r — Easy Peasy

1) You'll probably remember about relative atomic mass from page 45.

2) You can find relative atomic mass (A_r) numbers by looking at the periodic table.
The bigger number for each element is its relative atomic mass.
For example:

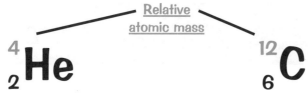

Relative atomic mass

$$^4_2He \qquad ^{12}_6C$$

Relative Formula Mass, M_r — Also Easy Peasy

'M_r' is just a shorter way of
saying 'relative formula mass'.

1) Every compound has a relative formula mass.

2) It's just all the relative atomic masses of the elements in the compound added together.

3) E.g. for $MgCl_2$ you add up the A_r of Mg, Cl and another Cl:

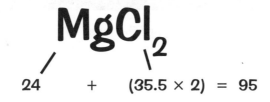

$$MgCl_2$$

$$24 \quad + \quad (35.5 \times 2) = 95$$

So the M_r for $MgCl_2$
is simply 95.

4) In the exam you'll probably be given the A_r values you need in the question. Here's another example:

> Question: Find the relative formula mass for calcium hydroxide, $Ca(OH)_2$, using the given data:
> A_r for Ca = 40 A_r for O = 16 A_r for H = 1

ANSWER:

$$Ca(OH)_2$$

The small 2 means everything in the
brackets. So, 2 Os AND two Hs.

$$40 + (2 \times 16) + (2 \times 1) = 74$$

So the M_r for
$Ca(OH)_2$ is 74.

Numbers? — and you thought you were doing chemistry...

So relative formula mass — hopefully not as bad as you thought it was going to be. Just make sure you know
exactly how many atoms of each thing you have before you start. Also watch out for the atoms in brackets —
like in the $Ca(OH)_2$ example above. Anyway, for a bit of practice, try this question:
Find the relative formula mass of these compounds: NaOH, Fe_2O_3, $MgSO_4$
Answers on page 108.

Percentage Composition By Mass

Bad news — this page is full of <u>maths</u>. Good news — if you learn the <u>formula</u> then it shouldn't be too bad. You'll need to know how to work out relative formula mass first though — so flick back and have another look at the <u>previous page</u> if you aren't sure.

Calculating % Composition by Mass of Elements in a Compound

Make sure you learn this formula:

The composition of a compound is just the elements that make it up, e.g. water (H_2O) is composed of hydrogen and oxygen.

$$\text{Percentage mass OF AN ELEMENT IN A COMPOUND} = \frac{A_r \times \text{No. of atoms (of that element)}}{M_r \text{ (of whole compound)}} \times 100$$

EXAMPLE 1: Find the percentage mass of magnesium in magnesium oxide, MgO.

ANSWER:

A_r of magnesium = 24, A_r of oxygen = 16

M_r of MgO = 24 + 16 = 40

Now use the formula:

There's only 1 atom of magnesium in MgO, so this number is 1.

$$\text{Percentage Mass} = \frac{A_r \times \text{No. of atoms}}{M_r} \times 100 = \frac{24 \times 1}{40} \times 100 = 60\%$$

That's all there is to it. Magnesium makes up <u>60%</u> of the mass of magnesium oxide.

By using the same method you can work out the % of oxygen in MgO as well.

EXAMPLE 2: Find the percentage mass of sodium in sodium carbonate, Na_2CO_3.

ANSWER:

A_r of sodium = 23, A_r of carbon = 12, A_r of oxygen = 16

M_r of Na_2CO_3 = (2 × 23) + 12 + (3 × 16) = 106

There are two sodium atoms in Na_2CO_3 so you have to multiply 23 by 2 here.

$$\text{Percentage Mass} = \frac{A_r \times \text{No. of atoms}}{M_r} \times 100 = \frac{23 \times 2}{106} \times 100 = 43.4\%$$

Sodium makes up <u>43.4%</u> of the mass of sodium carbonate.

Mass composition — I think that's what they used to call 'heavy rock'...

Make sure that <u>formula</u> is stuck in your brain before you go anywhere near that exam hall because you can't work this stuff out without it. Here's another annoying question — but it's for your own good:

What is the mass composition of bromine in calcium bromide, $CaBr_2$? *Answers on page 108.*

Empirical Formulas

Hopefully you're in the mood for more <u>maths</u> — because this page is filled with it (groans...).

Finding the Empirical Formula

1) The <u>empirical formula</u> of a compound is its <u>simplest formula</u>.

2) For example, <u>propene</u>, C_3H_6, would have the empirical formula <u>CH_2</u> (divide by 3).

3) The empirical formula can be calculated from the <u>masses</u> of elements that react to make a compound.

This sounds a lot worse than it really is. These are the steps you need:

> 1) <u>List all the elements</u> in the compound (there's usually only two or three!)
> 2) <u>Underneath them</u>, write their <u>masses</u>. (You'll be given these in the question.)
> 3) <u>Divide</u> each mass <u>by the A_r</u> for that particular element.
> 4) Turn the numbers you get into <u>a whole number ratio</u>.
> 5) When the ratio is in its <u>simplest form</u>, this tells you the empirical formula of the compound.

Example 1: Find the empirical formula of the magnesium oxide produced when 9.6 g of magnesium react with 6.4 g of oxygen. (A_r for magnesium = 24, A_r for oxygen = 16)

Method:

1) List the two elements: Mg   O

2) Write in the reacting masses: 9.6   6.4

3) Divide by the A_r for each element: $\frac{9.6}{24} = 0.4$ $\frac{6.4}{16} = 0.4$

At this point you don't have whole numbers — the easiest way to get them is to multiply by 10 so they both equal 4.

4) Multiply by 10...   4   :   4

The formula is now Mg_4O_4. Divide both numbers by 4 to get the empirical (simplest) formula — MgO.

5) ...then divide by 4   1   :   1

So the simplest formula is 1 atom of Mg to 1 atom of O, i.e. MgO. And that's it done.

Example 2: Find the empirical formula of the compound made when 2.4 g of carbon react with 0.8 g of hydrogen. (A_r for carbon = 12, A_r for hydrogen = 1)

Method:

1) List the two elements: C   H

2) Write in the reacting masses: 2.4   0.8

3) Divide by the A_r for each element: $\frac{2.4}{12} = 0.2$ $\frac{0.8}{1} = 0.8$

4) Multiply by 10...   2   :   8

5) ...then divide by 2   1   :   4

So the simplest formula is 1 atom of C to 4 atoms of H, i.e. CH_4.

The 'simplest formula' — doesn't look very simple to me...

Make sure you learn the <u>five rules</u> in the red box. Then try this question: Answer on page 108.

Find the empirical formula of the compound formed when 84 g of nitrogen react with 18 g of hydrogen.

Percentage Yield

Percentage yield tells you about the <u>overall success</u> of an experiment. It compares what you think you should get (<u>theoretical yield</u>) with what you get in practice (<u>actual yield</u>).

Percentage Yield Compares Actual and Theoretical Yield

1) The <u>yield</u> of a reaction is the <u>mass</u> of <u>product</u> made in the reaction.

2) Scientists can work out how much product they'd <u>expect</u> to get in a reaction. This is called the <u>theoretical yield</u> of the reaction.

3) The <u>actual yield</u> is the amount of product you end up getting. It's usually <u>lower</u> then the theoretical yield.

4) The <u>percentage yield</u> compares the actual yield with the theoretical yield. It's given by the <u>formula</u>:

$$\text{percentage yield} = \frac{\text{actual yield (grams)}}{\text{theoretical yield (grams)}} \times 100$$

5) Percentage yield is <u>always</u> somewhere between 0 and 100%. A <u>100% yield</u> means that you got <u>all</u> the product <u>you expected</u> to get. A <u>0% yield</u> means that <u>no product</u> at all was made.

> <u>Example:</u> The theoretical yield of a reaction was 2.7 g. The actual yield was 1.2 g. What was the percentage yield of the reaction?
>
> <u>Answer:</u>
>
> $$\text{percentage yield} = \frac{\text{actual yield (grams)}}{\text{theoretical yield (grams)}} \times 100 = \frac{1.2}{2.7} \times 100 = 44.4\%$$

Yields are Always Less Than 100%

In real life, you <u>never</u> get a 100% yield. Here's why:

1) <u>Incomplete reactions</u> — if not all of the <u>reactants</u> are <u>turned</u> into product, the reaction is incomplete. The yield will be lower than expected.

2) <u>Practical losses</u> — you always lose a bit when you move chemicals from one container to another. E.g. when you move a <u>liquid</u> to a new container — some of it always gets left behind on the <u>inside surface</u> of the old container.

3) <u>Unwanted reactions</u> — things don't always go exactly to plan. Sometimes unexpected reactions happen. This means the yield of the <u>product</u> you actually want goes down.

Waste in Reactions Costs Money

1) If you're making <u>lots of waste</u>, that's a <u>problem</u>. Reactions that make lots of waste don't usually make very much money. This is because waste products usually <u>aren't commercially useful</u> (they can't be sold to make money).

2) Getting rid of waste products <u>safely</u> can be <u>very expensive</u>. If a waste product is <u>harmful</u>, it can be a threat to <u>people</u> and the <u>environment</u>.

You can't always get what you want...

A high percentage yield means there's <u>not much waste</u> — which is good for keeping <u>costs down</u>. For a reaction to be used in industry it needs to have a high percentage yield. Or reactants that can be used again and again.

Revision Summary for C2b Topics 4, 5 & 6

I don't know about you but I'm pretty glad that section is over. But don't get too excited — I have filled this page with some lovely questions for you to have a go at. Don't just ignore them and keep going — doing them until you get them right is the only way you know for sure that you've learnt this stuff.

1) Give two normal properties of metals.

2) Describe the structure of a metal.

3) Is this statement true or false? "Alkali metals have high melting points."

4) Potassium is a Group 1 element. When placed in water, potassium reacts quickly.
   What gas is made by this reaction?

5) What colour is bromine at room temperature?

6) Do hydrogen halides dissolve in water to form acidic or alkaline solutions?

7) Name two noble gases and state a use for each.

8) Is this true or false? "The boiling point of the noble gases decreases as you go down the group."

9) What is an exothermic reaction? Give two examples.

10) Give two examples of an endothermic reaction.

11) How would you measure the temperature change during a neutralisation reaction?

12) What are the four factors that affect the rate of a reaction?

13) A student carries out an experiment to measure the effect of surface area on the
    reaction between marble chips and hydrochloric acid. He used three different samples of marble chips.
    Sample A – 10 g of small marble chips
    Sample B – 10 g of large marble chips
    Sample C – 10 g of powdered marble
    Which sample would have produced the fastest reaction?

14) What is the effect of increasing temperature on the rate of a reaction?

15) What is a catalyst?

16) What is the role of a catalytic converter in car exhausts?

17)* Find M_r for each of these: a) CO_2 b) $MgCO_3$ c) ZnO
    (A_r for C = 12, A_r for O = 16, A_r for Mg = 24, A_r for Zn = 65)

18)* Calculate the percentage by mass of nitrogen in $NaNO_3$.
    (A_r for Na = 23, A_r for N = 14, A_r for O = 16)

19)* Find the empirical formula of the compound formed when 240 g of calcium reacts with 228 g of fluorine.
    (A_r for Ca = 40, A_r for F = 19)

20) a) What is the formula for percentage yield?
    b) How does percentage yield differ from actual yield?

21) Give two reasons why the percentage yield of a reaction could be less than 100%.

* Answers on page 108

Static Electricity

Static electricity is all about charges which <u>can't</u> move. But before that we need to look at the atom...

Atoms *Have a* Nucleus in the Middle *with* Electrons Moving Round It

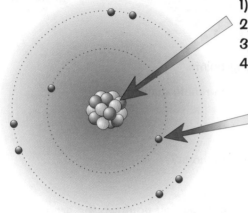

1) The <u>nucleus</u> is <u>tiny</u> but it makes up most of the <u>mass</u> of the atom.
2) It contains <u>protons</u> which are <u>positively charged</u> (+).
3) It also contains <u>neutrons</u> which are <u>neutral</u> (have no charge).
4) The nucleus has an overall <u>positive charge</u>.

5) The rest of the atom is mostly <u>empty space</u>.
6) The <u>negative electrons</u> move round the outside of the nucleus really fast.
7) They give the atom its <u>size</u>.
8) But they have almost <u>no</u> mass.
9) Here are the relative <u>charges</u> and <u>masses</u> of each particle:

PARTICLE	MASS	CHARGE
Proton	1	+1
Neutron	1	0
Electron	$\frac{1}{2000}$	-1

Build-up of Static *is Caused by* Friction

1) When two <u>insulating</u> materials are <u>rubbed</u> together, <u>friction</u> causes <u>electrons</u> to be <u>scraped off one</u> and <u>dumped</u> on the other.
2) This leaves a <u>positive</u> (+) charge on one because <u>electrons</u> (-) have been <u>lost</u>.
3) It leaves a <u>negative</u> (-) charge on the other because <u>electrons</u> have been <u>gained</u>.

Charges that aren't moving are called electrostatic charges or static electricity.

Examples: Dusting rods

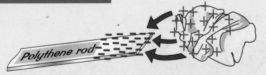

With a <u>polythene rod</u>, electrons move <u>from the duster</u> to the rod. The <u>rod</u> becomes <u>negatively charged</u> and the <u>duster</u> is left with an <u>equal positive charge</u>.

With an <u>acetate rod</u>, electrons move <u>from the rod</u> to the duster. The <u>duster</u> becomes <u>negatively charged</u> and the <u>rod</u> is left with an <u>equal positive charge</u>.

Like *Charges Repel,* Unlike *Charges Attract*

1) Two things with <u>opposite</u> charges (positive and negative) are <u>attracted</u> to each other.
2) Two things with the <u>same</u> charge will <u>repel</u> each other (push each other away).

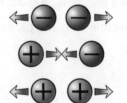

Static caravans — where electrons go on holiday...

So, insulators can be charged by friction, through the transfer of electrons. And this leaves one material negatively charged and the other positively charged. Which way the electrons move depends on the two materials. Yup.

Static Electricity

You might not realise it, but we often experience static electricity in our <u>everyday lives</u>. It's shocking stuff.

Static Electricity can Cause <u>Little Sparks</u> or <u>Shocks</u>

1) Static charge can build up between your <u>clothes</u> and a <u>car seat</u>.

2) <u>Friction</u> between the two means <u>electrons</u> are <u>scraped off</u> one onto the other.

3) When you get out of the car and touch the <u>metal door</u>, the charge can <u>flow</u> between your clothes and the ground.

4) The <u>movement</u> of <u>charge</u> gives you a <u>shock</u>.

5) You can get shocks from door handles in a similar way:

- If you walk on a <u>nylon carpet</u> wearing shoes with <u>insulating soles</u> (like rubber), static charge will <u>build up</u> on your body.
- If you touch a <u>metal door handle</u>, the charge flows and you get a <u>little shock</u>.

Some <u>Charged</u> Objects can <u>Attract</u> Other Objects

Balloons can <u>Stick to</u> Walls

1) <u>Electrons</u> can be transferred to a <u>balloon</u> by <u>rubbing</u> it against your <u>clothes</u>.

2) This leaves it with a <u>negative charge</u>.

3) If you hold it against a <u>wall</u> it will <u>stick</u> — even though the wall <u>isn't</u> charged.

4) That's because the charges on the <u>surface</u> of the wall can <u>move</u> a little — the <u>negative charges</u> on the balloon <u>repel</u> the negative charges on the surface of the wall.

5) This leaves a <u>positive charge</u> on the surface — which <u>attracts</u> the <u>negatively charged</u> balloon and <u>holds</u> it on the wall.

6) Using a <u>charged</u> object to force the charges in an <u>uncharged object</u> to <u>move</u> is called <u>induction</u>.

A <u>Charged Comb</u> can <u>Pick Up Small Pieces</u> of Paper

1) Running a <u>comb</u> through your hair transfers <u>electrons</u> to the comb, leaving it <u>negatively charged</u>.

2) It can then be used to <u>pick up</u> little pieces of <u>paper</u>, even though they have <u>no charge</u>.

3) This is because the negatively charged comb <u>repels electrons in the paper</u>, which causes <u>induction</u> of a <u>positive charge</u> on the surface of the paper.

4) Because they have <u>opposite charges</u>, the paper and the comb are <u>attracted</u> to one another.

Lightning <u>is also Caused by a</u> <u>Build-Up</u> of <u>Static Charge</u>

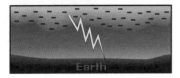

1) Rain drops and ice can <u>bump together</u> inside a storm cloud knocking off <u>electrons</u>.

2) This leaves the <u>top</u> of the cloud <u>positively charged</u> and the <u>bottom</u> of the cloud <u>negative</u>.

3) This creates a <u>huge voltage</u>. You get a <u>big spark</u> of lightning when the negative charges suddenly flow to the ground.

I know, I know — yet another shocking joke...

Learn all the everyday <u>examples</u> of static electicity above. Then rub your head against a balloon as a reward.

Uses and Dangers of Static Electricity

Static electricity can be a bit <u>annoying</u> sometimes, but it also has some <u>good uses</u>.

Paint Sprayers Use Electrostatic Charges to get an Even Coat

1) Bikes and cars are painted using <u>electrostatic paint sprayers</u>.
2) The spray gun is <u>charged</u>, which charges up the small drops of <u>paint</u>.
3) Each paint drop <u>repels</u> all the others, since they've all got the <u>same charge</u>, so you get a very <u>fine spray</u>.
4) The object to be painted is given an <u>opposite charge</u> to the gun.
5) This <u>attracts</u> the fine spray of paint.
6) This gives an <u>even coat</u>, and hardly any paint is <u>wasted</u>.
7) Also, parts of the bike or car pointing <u>away</u> from the spray gun <u>still get paint</u>.
8) Many other electrostatic sprayers work in exactly the <u>same way</u>, such as <u>insecticide sprayers</u>.

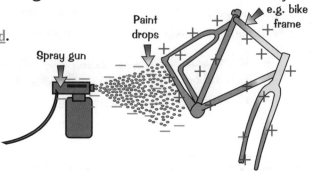

Spray gun | Paint drops | Object, e.g. bike frame

Just Say No To Electrostatic Sprayers

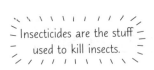

Insecticides are the stuff used to kill insects.

Electrostatic Charges can Cause a Fuel Filling Nightmare

1) As <u>fuel</u> flows out of a <u>filler pipe</u> into, say, an <u>aircraft</u> or <u>tanker</u>, then <u>static charge can build up</u>.
2) This can lead to a <u>spark</u> which might cause an <u>explosion</u> in <u>dusty</u> or <u>fumey</u> places (such as <u>inside the fuel tank</u>).

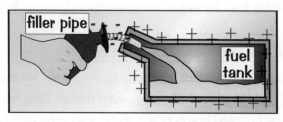

filler pipe | fuel tank

3) These <u>sparks</u> can be <u>prevented</u> by <u>earthing</u> the charged object.
4) This means connecting it to the <u>ground</u> using a <u>conductor</u> (such as a copper wire).
5) <u>Earthing</u> gives an <u>easy route</u> for the static charges to travel into the ground.
6) This means <u>no charge</u> can <u>build up</u> to give you a shock or make a spark.
7) The <u>electrons</u> flow <u>down</u> the conductor to the ground if the charge is <u>negative</u>.
8) They flow <u>up</u> the conductor from the ground if the charge is <u>positive</u>.
9) <u>Fuel tankers</u> must be <u>earthed</u> to avoid sparks that might cause the fuel to <u>explode</u>.

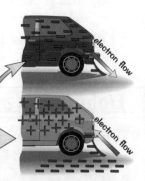

electron flow

That page really brought me back down to Earth...

Scary stuff. Remember that <u>earthing</u> stops lots of charge building up in once place so there aren't any sparks — which is really important for fuelling aircraft etc. Hmm, let's hope the next page is a bit more cheery.

Charge and Current

This page is all about charges <u>moving</u> in an <u>electrical circuit</u>. If you're worried that reading it might harm your street cred, then let me tell you that it's all <u>current</u>. Ho, ho.

Electric Current *is the Rate of Flow of Charge*

1) Current is the <u>rate of flow of charge</u> (how <u>quickly</u> the charge moves).

2) In a <u>metal</u>, the current is a flow of <u>electrons</u>.

3) The <u>amount</u> of <u>charge</u> flowing past a point in a circuit depends on the <u>current</u> and the length of <u>time</u> it flows for:

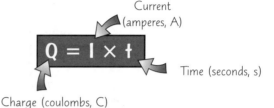

When you earth a charged conductor (p.78), a current flows.

$$\text{Charge} = \text{Current} \times \text{Time}$$

$$Q = I \times t$$

Current (amperes, A)

Time (seconds, s)

Charge (coulombs, C)

Example

<u>EXAMPLE</u>: A battery charger passes a current of 2.5 A through a battery for 4 hours. How much charge does the charger transfer to the battery?

<u>ANSWER</u>: First, change 4 hours into seconds:
$4 \times 60 \times 60 = 14\ 400$ s
so, $Q = I \times t = 2.5$ A $\times 14\ 400$ s $= 36\ 000$ C

Cells *and Batteries Supply Direct Current*

1) <u>Cells</u> and <u>batteries</u> can be used in an electrical circuit to supply <u>direct current</u> (d.c.).

2) Direct current is a current that keeps flowing in the <u>same direction</u>.

3) This means that the <u>charge</u> moves in <u>one direction</u> only.

4) You can also get <u>alternating current</u> (a.c.).

5) This is current that <u>changes direction</u>.

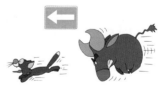

Finding it hard to revise charge and current? Don't QIT it yet...

Make sure you know how to <u>use</u> the equation above. Don't forget that the symbol for current is <u>I</u> and the symbol for charge is <u>Q</u>. Barmy. Learn all the definitions too, like electric current being the rate of flow of charge.

Electric Current and Potential Difference

You'll have heard the words <u>current</u>, <u>voltage</u> and <u>resistance</u> loads of times before. But because I'm so nice, here's a <u>reminder</u> of what they all mean. You can thank me later. Make sure you know them...

Current in a Circuit Depends on Potential Difference

1) Current is the rate of <u>flow</u> of charge round a circuit. Unit: ampere, A.

2) Potential difference is the <u>driving force</u> that pushes the current round. Unit: volt, V.

3) Resistance is anything in the circuit which <u>slows the flow down</u>. Unit: ohm, Ω.

> Potential difference is just another name for <u>voltage</u> — they both mean the <u>same thing</u>.

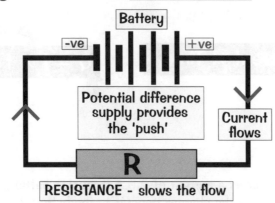

Battery

−ve +ve

Potential difference supply provides the 'push'

Current flows

R

RESISTANCE - slows the flow

4) There's a balance: the <u>potential difference</u> is trying to <u>push</u> the current round the circuit, and the <u>resistance</u> is <u>slowing</u> it down. The <u>size</u> of the <u>current</u> depends on the size of <u>potential difference</u> and <u>resistance</u>:

> If you <u>increase the potential difference</u> — then <u>more current</u> will flow.
> If you <u>increase the resistance</u> — then <u>less current</u> will flow
> (or <u>a higher potential difference</u> will be needed to keep the <u>same current</u> flowing).

Current is Conserved at a Junction

1) In a <u>parallel circuit</u> (like the one below) each <u>component</u> is <u>separately</u> connected to the power <u>supply</u>.

2) There are <u>junctions</u> where the current either <u>splits</u> or <u>rejoins</u>.

3) Current <u>doesn't</u> get <u>used up</u> or <u>lost</u> in a circuit — it is <u>conserved</u>.

4) So, current at a <u>junction</u> is conserved.

5) The total current <u>entering</u> a <u>junction</u> is <u>equal</u> to the <u>total current leaving</u> a junction.

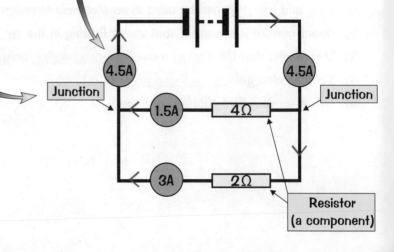

Junction

4.5A   **4.5A**

Junction

1.5A   **4Ω**

3A   **2Ω**

Resistor (a component)

Another example of a split.
N.B. You won't be tested on this.

I'm always conserved at road junctions...

...which means I'm often late for work. Maybe I should just take the bus. It's really important that you get the definitions for <u>potential difference</u> and <u>current</u> clear in your head. They pop up lots on the next couple of pages.

Resistance and V = I × R

Ooh experiments, you've got to love them. Here's a <u>simple experiment</u> for looking at resistance...

The Standard Test Circuit

The circuit below is a very basic circuit used for testing <u>components</u>.

Components are devices you use in electric circuits, such as light bulbs, motors and resistors.

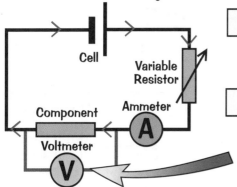

Cell
Variable Resistor
Component
Ammeter
Voltmeter

The Ammeter:

1) Measures the <u>current</u> (in <u>amperes</u>) flowing through the component.
2) Must be placed <u>in series</u> (connected in a line) with the component.

The Voltmeter:

1) Measures the <u>potential difference</u> (in <u>volts</u>) across the component.
2) Must be placed <u>in parallel</u> around the <u>component</u> being tested — <u>NOT</u> around the variable resistor or the cell.

Looking at the Link Between Potential Difference, Current and Resistance

1) We can use the test circuit above to look at the <u>link</u> between <u>potential difference</u> (voltage), <u>current</u> and <u>resistance</u>.
2) The <u>component</u>, the <u>ammeter</u> and the <u>variable resistor</u> are all in <u>series</u> — which means they can be put in <u>any order</u> in the main circuit.
3) The <u>voltmeter</u> can <u>ONLY</u> be placed <u>in parallel</u> around the <u>COMPONENT under test</u>, as shown.
4) The <u>variable resistor</u> is used to <u>change</u> the <u>resistance</u> in the <u>circuit</u>.
5) Changing the resistance of the <u>variable resistor</u> changes the size of the <u>current</u> (see p. 80).
6) This lets you take <u>pairs of readings</u> from the <u>ammeter</u> and <u>voltmeter</u>.
7) You can then <u>plot</u> these values for <u>current</u> and <u>potential difference</u> on a <u>graph</u> (see next page).

There's an Equation Linking Potential Difference and Current

You need to know how to use this equation:

Potential Difference = Current × Resistance

Potential difference (volts, V)
$$V = I \times R$$
Resistance (ohms, Ω)
Current (amperes, A)

<u>EXAMPLE:</u> A 4 Ω resistor in a circuit has a current of 1.5 A flowing through it. What is the potential difference across the resistor?

<u>ANSWER:</u> Using the equation V = I × R:
V = 1.5 A × 4 Ω = <u>6 V</u>

The missing link.

Knowing your left from your right — another standard test...

Make sure you know what an ammeter and voltmeter are used for, and where they go in a circuit.

Electrical Devices and Resistance

Some resistors have a <u>fixed</u> resistance (it is always the <u>same</u>). Others can <u>change</u> their resistance.

Three Important Graphs to Learn

These graphs show how <u>current</u> varies with <u>potential difference</u> for each type of device:

Fixed Resistors

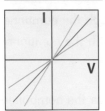

At a constant temperature, <u>current</u> is <u>proportional to potential difference</u> (I increases as V increases).

<u>Different resistors</u> have different <u>resistances</u> — this is why there are different <u>lines</u>.

Filament Lamp

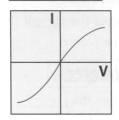

As the <u>temperature</u> of the filament <u>increases</u>, the <u>resistance</u> <u>increases</u>. **This is why the graph <u>curves</u>.**

Diode

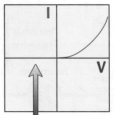

Current will only flow through a <u>diode</u> <u>in one direction</u>, as shown.

No current can flow in this direction no matter what the voltage is.

Light-Dependent Resistor or "LDR"

1) A <u>light-dependent resistor</u> or <u>LDR</u> is a special type of resistor that <u>changes</u> its resistance depending on how much <u>light</u> there is.

2) In <u>bright light</u>, the resistance is <u>low</u>.

3) In <u>darkness</u>, the resistance is <u>high</u>.

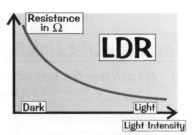

Thermistor (Temperature-Dependent Resistor)

1) The resistance of a <u>thermistor</u> depends on <u>temperature</u>.

2) In <u>hot</u> conditions, the resistance is <u>low</u>.

3) In <u>cool</u> conditions, the resistance is <u>high</u>.

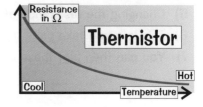

Resistors Get Hot When an Electric Current Passes Through Them

1) When there is an <u>electric current</u> in a <u>resistor</u> there is an <u>energy transfer</u> which <u>heats the resistor</u>.

2) This energy transfer is due to <u>particles colliding</u> in the resistor.

This heating effect has <u>disadvantages</u> and <u>advantages</u>:

1) It increases the resistor's <u>resistance</u> — so <u>less</u> or <u>no current</u> will flow.

2) It can make circuits <u>less efficient</u> — as some energy is <u>wasted</u> as <u>heat</u>.

3) <u>Components</u> in the circuit may <u>melt</u> — which means the circuit will <u>stop</u> working, or <u>not work properly</u>.

4) <u>Fuses</u> use this effect to <u>protect</u> circuits — they <u>melt</u> and <u>break</u> the circuit if the current gets <u>too high</u>.

5) <u>Toasters</u> contain a coil of wire with a really <u>high</u> resistance. When a current passes through the coil, its <u>temperature increases</u> so much that it <u>glows</u> and gives off heat radiation which <u>cooks</u> the bread.

6) <u>Filament lamps</u> work in a similar way to toasters — the <u>glowing</u> is the light you see.

Cheese on toast and Sunday roast — advantages of the heating effect

Remember the <u>shapes</u> of the graphs for the <u>fixed resistors</u>, <u>filament lamp</u> and <u>diode</u> — the examiners love them.

Electrical Power and Energy

Electric appliances (like TVs or drills) <u>transfer energy</u> from one type to another.
How <u>quickly</u> the appliance transfers this energy depends on its <u>power</u>...

Electrical Power _is the_ Rate _an Appliance_ Transfers Energy

1) An appliance with a <u>high power rating</u> transfers a <u>lot</u> of <u>energy</u> in a <u>short time</u>.

2) This energy comes from the <u>current</u> flowing through it.

3) The equation for <u>electrical power</u> is:

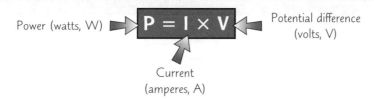

ELECTRICAL POWER = CURRENT × POTENTIAL DIFFERENCE

Power (watts, W) → $P = I \times V$ ← Potential difference (volts, V)

Current (amperes, A)

<u>EXAMPLE</u>: A hairdryer is attached to a <u>230 V</u> mains electricity supply.
When it is turned on, the hairdryer has a current of <u>5 A</u> flowing through.
Calculate the <u>power</u> of the hairdryer.

<u>ANSWER</u>: Use $P = I \times V = 5\,A \times 230\,V = \underline{1150\,W}$

The _Energy Transferred_ by an Appliance _Depends_ on _Three_ Things

1) The <u>energy transferred</u> by an appliance depends on:
   - the <u>current</u> through it
   - the <u>potential difference</u> supplied to it
   - <u>how long</u> it is on for.

2) The equation for energy transferred is:

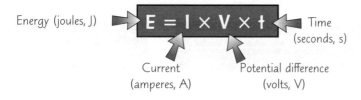

ENERGY TRANSFERRED = CURRENT × POTENTIAL DIFFERENCE × TIME

Energy (joules, J) → $E = I \times V \times t$ ← Time (seconds, s)

Current (amperes, A)   Potential difference (volts, V)

<u>EXAMPLE</u>: An electric toothbrush has a <u>3 V</u> battery. A current of <u>0.8 A</u> flows through it for <u>3 minutes</u>.
Calculate the energy transferred by the motor.

<u>ANSWER</u>: First, change 3 minutes into seconds: $3 \times 60 = 180\,s$
So, $E = I \times V \times t = 0.8\,A \times 3\,V \times 180\,s = \underline{432\,J}$

The difference between power and energy? Just a little time...

Crikey, a page all about equations — make sure you know how to use <u>both</u> of them. If you're asked to work out the energy transferred by an appliance, don't forget to <u>convert</u> the time into <u>seconds</u> (if it isn't in seconds already).

Velocity and Acceleration

Did you know that speed, velocity and acceleration are different things? Crazy. Read all about it below.

Speed and Velocity — HOW FAST YOU'RE GOING

1) Speed and velocity are both measured in m/s (or km/h or mph).
2) They both say how fast you're going.
3) But there's a difference between them which you need to know:

> SPEED is just how fast you're going — the direction doesn't matter.
> VELOCITY must also have the DIRECTION given.
> The distance travelled in a particular direction is called the DISPLACEMENT.

4) For example, your speed might be 30 mph, but your velocity would be 30 mph north.
5) Velocity and displacement are called vector quantities — they have magnitude (size) and direction.

Speed, Distance and Time — the Equation:

Use this equation to work out speed:

$$\text{Speed (m/s)} = \frac{\text{Distance (m)}}{\text{Time (s)}} \qquad s = \frac{d}{t}$$

EXAMPLE: A cat walks 20 m in 40 s. Find its speed.
ANSWER: $s = d/t = 20 \text{ m} / 40 \text{ s} = \underline{0.5 \text{ m/s}}$

If you're asked to calculate a velocity in the exam, don't forget to say what direction it's in.

Acceleration comes from a Change in Speed or Direction

1) Acceleration is how quickly the velocity is changing.
2) This change in velocity can be a CHANGE IN SPEED or a CHANGE IN DIRECTION or both.
3) Acceleration is a vector quantity like velocity — it has magnitude (size) and direction.
4) Use this equation to work out acceleration:

$$\text{Acceleration (m/s}^2) = \frac{\text{Change in Velocity (m/s)}}{\text{Time taken (s)}} \qquad a = \frac{(v - u)}{t}$$

Here, u is the initial velocity of the object (its velocity at the start) and v is its final velocity.

There are two tricky things with this equation:
- The '(v − u)', which means working out the 'change in velocity'.
- The unit of acceleration, which is m/s². (Don't get confused with the units for velocity, m/s).

EXAMPLE: A cat accelerates from 2 m/s to 6 m/s in 5 s. Find its acceleration.
ANSWER: $a = (v - u) / t = (6 - 2) / 5 = 4 \div 5 = \underline{0.8 \text{ m/s}^2}$

They say a change in velocity is as good as a rest...

Lots of facts to remember there, but it's all important stuff. Make sure you've learnt it all before you move on. Remember — displacement, velocity and acceleration are all vector quantities because they have size and direction.

D-T and V-T Graphs

Learn all these details real good. Make sure you can tell the <u>two types of graph</u> apart.

Distance-Time (D-T) Graphs

A <u>D-T graph</u> shows how far something has travelled over time.

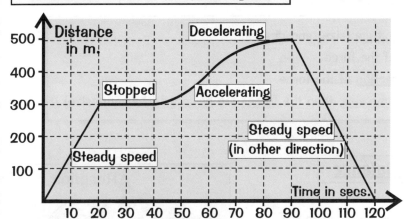

1) <u>Gradient (steepness) = speed</u>.
2) The <u>steeper</u> the graph, the <u>faster</u> it's going.
3) <u>Flat</u> sections are where it's <u>stopped</u>.
4) <u>Downhill</u> sections mean it's <u>going back</u> towards its starting point.
5) <u>Curves</u> show <u>acceleration</u> (speeding up) or <u>deceleration</u> (slowing down).
6) A <u>steepening</u> curve means it's <u>speeding up</u> (increasing gradient).
7) A <u>levelling off</u> curve means it's <u>slowing down</u> (decreasing gradient).

Calculating speed from a distance-time graph

The <u>speed</u> of the object on the <u>first section</u> of the graph is:

$$\text{Speed} = \text{gradient} = \frac{\text{vertical } (\uparrow)}{\text{horizontal } (\rightarrow)} = \frac{300 \text{ m}}{20 \text{ s}} = \underline{15 \text{ m/s}}$$

Don't forget that you have to use the <u>scales</u> of the axes to work out the gradient. <u>Don't</u> measure in <u>cm</u>!

Velocity-Time (V-T) Graphs

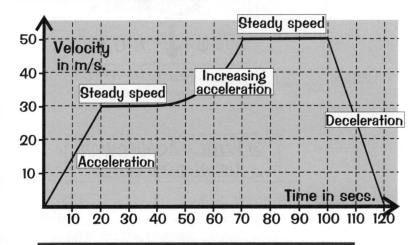

1) <u>Gradient = acceleration</u>.
2) The <u>steeper</u> the graph, the <u>greater</u> the <u>acceleration</u> or deceleration.
3) <u>Flat</u> sections show <u>steady speed</u>.
4) <u>Uphill</u> sections (/) are <u>acceleration</u>.
5) <u>Downhill</u> sections (\) are <u>deceleration</u>.
6) A <u>curve</u> means <u>changing acceleration</u>.

Calculating acceleration from a velocity-time graph

The <u>acceleration</u> of the object on the <u>first section</u> of the graph is:

$$\text{Acceleration} = \text{gradient} = \frac{\text{vertical } (\uparrow)}{\text{horizontal } (\rightarrow)} = \frac{30 \text{ m/s}}{20 \text{ s}} = \underline{1.5 \text{ m/s}^2}$$

Understanding graphs — it can be a real uphill struggle...

The tricky thing about these two types of graph is that they can look pretty much the same. Learn all the points, and whenever you're reading a motion graph, <u>check the axis labels</u> carefully so you know which type of graph it is.

Forces

A <u>force</u> is simply a <u>push</u> or a <u>pull</u>. We can draw <u>force diagrams</u> to show the forces <u>acting on</u> an object.

Four Important Things to Remember About Force Diagrams:

1) Force is a <u>vector quantity</u> — it has <u>magnitude</u> (size) and <u>direction</u>.
2) The <u>length</u> of the arrow shows the <u>size</u> of the force.
3) The <u>direction</u> of the arrow shows the <u>direction</u> of the force.
4) If the arrows in <u>opposite pairs</u> are the <u>same size</u>, then the <u>forces</u> are <u>balanced</u> (the same size).

1) Stationary Object — All Forces in Balance

1) Weight acts <u>downwards</u> (see p. 87).
2) This causes a <u>REACTION FORCE</u> from the surface <u>pushing</u> the object <u>back up</u>. This is the <u>only way</u> it can be in <u>BALANCE</u>.
3) On the diagram, this is shown by the <u>length</u> of the <u>reaction</u> and <u>weight</u> arrows being the <u>same size</u> and in <u>opposite</u> directions.

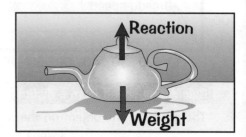

2) Steady Horizontal Velocity — All Forces in Balance

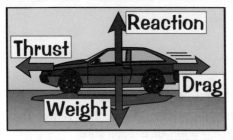

To move with a <u>steady speed</u> the forces must be in <u>balance</u>. (Look at the length and direction of the arrows.)

3) Steady Vertical Velocity — All Forces in Balance

This skydiver is free-falling at '<u>terminal velocity</u>' — see next page.

Resultant Force = 700 N - 700 N = 0 N. So there is no acceleration.

4) Horizontal Acceleration — Unbalanced Forces

1) You only get <u>acceleration</u> when there's an overall <u>resultant</u> (unbalanced) <u>force</u>.
2) This is shown on the diagrams by the length of one arrow being <u>longer</u> than the arrow in the <u>opposite</u> direction.
3) The <u>bigger</u> this <u>unbalanced force</u>, the <u>greater</u> the <u>acceleration</u> (see p. 89).

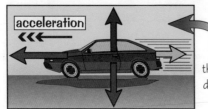

Note that the forces in the vertical (up and down) direction are still balanced.

5) Vertical Acceleration — Unbalanced Forces

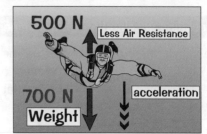

Resultant Force = 700 N - 500 N = 200 N. So there is an acceleration.

I thought skydiving was cool — but it's all about forces...

So, things <u>only accelerate</u> in a certain direction if there's an <u>overall force</u> in that direction. Simple.

Weight and Terminal Velocity

On the last page, we looked at <u>forces</u> acting on objects. Here's a bit more on one of those forces — <u>weight</u>.

Weight and Mass are Not the Same

1) <u>Weight</u> is a <u>force</u> measured in <u>newtons</u> (N). Weight is caused by the <u>pull</u> of gravity.

2) <u>Mass</u> is <u>not</u> a force — it is the <u>amount of 'stuff'</u> in an object. Mass is measured in <u>kilograms</u>.

3) An object has the <u>same</u> mass whether it's on <u>Earth</u> or on the <u>Moon</u> — but its <u>weight</u> will be <u>different</u>.

The Equation Linking Mass, Weight and Gravity

Weight (N) = mass (kg) × gravitational field strength (N/kg) $W = m \times g$

1) The letter g is the <u>strength</u> of the gravity — it's <u>different</u> for <u>different planets</u>, <u>moons</u> etc.

2) <u>On Earth</u> g is about <u>10 N/kg</u>. <u>On the Moon</u>, where the gravity is weaker, g is only about <u>1.6 N/kg</u>.

> <u>EXAMPLE</u>: What is the weight, in newtons, of a 5 kg mass, both on Earth and on the Moon?
> <u>ANSWER</u>: $W = m \times g$ On Earth: $W = 5 \times 10 = \underline{50\ N}$ (The weight of the 5 kg mass is 50 N.)
> On the Moon: $W = 5 \times 1.6 = \underline{8\ N}$ (The weight of the 5 kg mass is 8 N.)

Falling Objects in a Vacuum Accelerate at the Same Rate

1) <u>Gravity</u> makes <u>falling</u> objects <u>accelerate</u> (speed up).

2) In a <u>vacuum</u>, like space, gravity makes <u>all</u> objects <u>accelerate</u> at exactly the <u>same rate</u>.

3) So, on the <u>Moon</u>, hammers and feathers dropped at the <u>same time</u> will hit the ground <u>together</u>.

4) This is because there's <u>no air</u> in a vacuum — so there is no <u>air resistance</u> to slow down the falling objects.

5) But here on <u>Earth</u>, where there <u>is</u> air resistance, things are a little different...

Objects Falling Through Air Reach a Terminal Velocity

1) On Earth, when a falling object first <u>sets off</u> it has <u>much more</u> force (weight) <u>accelerating</u> it than <u>resistance</u> slowing it down.

2) This means it <u>speeds up</u>.

3) As its <u>speed</u> increases, the <u>air resistance</u> increases too.

4) This slowly <u>reduces</u> the <u>acceleration</u>.

5) Eventually the <u>air resistance</u> is <u>equal</u> to the <u>weight</u> of the falling object.

6) When these two forces are <u>balanced</u>, the object then <u>won't accelerate</u> any more.

7) It will have reached its maximum speed or <u>terminal velocity</u> and fall at a steady speed.

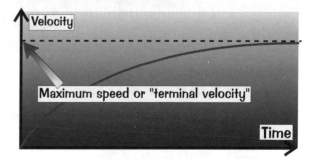
Velocity

Maximum speed or "terminal velocity"

Time

CGP health and safety tip #49 — beware of falling objects...

That sounded like a threat. It wasn't meant to be. Anyway, remember that all objects falling in a <u>vacuum</u> accelerate at the <u>same rate</u>. But that doesn't happen on Earth because of <u>air resistance</u>. I'm off to buy a helmet.

Forces and Motion

The next couple of pages have some important rules about <u>forces and motion</u>. Dust off your brain, folks.

When Two Bodies Interact They Exert a Force on Each Other

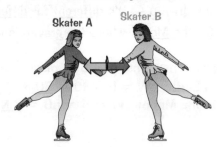

> If object A <u>exerts a force</u> on object B then object B exerts <u>the exact opposite force</u> on object A.

1) For example, if you <u>push</u> a trolley, the trolley will <u>push back</u> against you, with the <u>same sized force</u> in the <u>opposite direction</u>.

2) And as soon as you <u>stop</u> pushing, <u>so does the trolley</u>.

3) The force of you pushing the trolley is called the <u>action force</u>.

4) The force of the trolley pushing back against you is called the <u>reaction force</u> (see p.86).

5) Remember that the two forces are acting on <u>different objects</u>, so the objects can still <u>move</u>.

6) Think about a pair of ice skaters:

Skater A   Skater B

- When skater A pushes on skater B (the <u>action</u> force), she feels an equal and opposite force from skater B's hand (the <u>reaction</u> force).
- Both skaters feel the <u>same sized force</u>, BUT in <u>opposite directions</u>.
- The force makes them accelerate <u>away</u> from each other.

No Resultant Force Means No Change in Velocity

> If there is <u>zero resultant force</u> acting on an object (the forces are balanced) then the object will <u>remain at rest</u>, or else if it's already moving it'll just carry on at the <u>same velocity</u>.

A resultant force is the overall force acting on an object.

1) If something is <u>moving</u> at a <u>constant velocity</u>, or <u>isn't moving at all</u>, then the <u>forces</u> on it must all be <u>balanced</u>. There is <u>no resultant force</u>.

2) Things <u>DON'T NEED</u> a resultant force to <u>keep</u> them moving.

3) Remember — to keep going at a <u>steady speed</u>, there must be <u>ZERO</u> resultant force.

Steady speed and constant velocity mean the <u>same</u> thing.

Steady speed bus tours Ltd

I have a reaction to forces — they bring me out in a rash...

Ooh the stuff on that page is a bit tricky. Remember, when two objects touch, they exert an <u>equal and opposite</u> force on each other. Know what is meant by <u>action</u> and <u>reaction forces</u> too. And don't forget that if the resultant force on an object is <u>zero</u>, the object will either <u>remain still</u> or keeping going at a <u>constant velocity</u>.

Force and Acceleration

Now let's look at what happens if there <u>is</u> a <u>resultant force</u> on an object.   Hold on to your hats.

A Resultant Force Means Acceleration

> If the resultant force acting on an object is <u>not zero</u>, it will <u>accelerate</u> in the <u>direction</u> of the <u>resultant force</u>.

1) An <u>unbalanced</u> force will always produce <u>acceleration</u> (or deceleration).
2) This <u>acceleration</u> could be: <u>starting</u>, <u>stopping</u>, <u>speeding up</u>, <u>slowing down</u> or <u>changing direction</u>.
3) On a force diagram, the <u>arrows</u> will be <u>unequal</u>.
4) The bigger the <u>resultant force</u>, the <u>greater</u> the <u>acceleration</u> or <u>deceleration</u>.
5) The bigger the <u>mass</u> of the object, the <u>smaller the acceleration</u>.
6) To get a <u>big</u> mass to accelerate <u>as fast</u> as a <u>small</u> mass it needs a <u>bigger</u> resultant force.

There is an Equation for Resultant Force

$$\text{Force (N)} = \text{mass (kg)} \times \text{acceleration (m/s}^2)$$

$$F = m \times a$$

This is the resultant force.

<u>EXAMPLE</u>: A car of mass <u>1750 kg</u> accelerates at <u>3 m/s²</u>. Find the <u>resultant force</u> causing the acceleration.
<u>ANSWER</u>: $F = m \times a = 1750 \text{ kg} \times 3 \text{ m/s}^2 = \underline{\underline{5250 \text{ N}}}$

You can Investigate F = m × a Using a Trolley

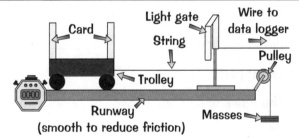

Card
Light gate
Wire to data logger
String
Pulley
Trolley
Runway (smooth to reduce friction)
Masses

1) Set up your equipment as shown to the left.
2) <u>Hold</u> the trolley and add a <u>100 g</u> mass to the end of the string, then <u>release</u> the trolley.
3) The 100 g mass pulls the trolley with a <u>constant force</u> so it <u>accelerates</u>.
4) The <u>light gate</u> detects <u>each</u> piece of card as it passes through it.
5) <u>Data logging software</u> works out the trolley's '<u>initial</u>' <u>velocity</u> (u) using the first card's width and the time it blocked the gate. The same is done with second piece of card to find the trolley's '<u>final</u>' <u>velocity</u> (v).
6) Record the <u>time</u> (t) it takes for the trolley to <u>pass through the gate</u> using the <u>stop clock</u>.
7) You can then work out the trolley's <u>acceleration</u> using $\underline{a = (\underline{v} - \underline{u}) \div \underline{t}}$ (p.84).
8) <u>Repeat</u> the experiment a few times to get an <u>average</u> acceleration.
9) Repeat the <u>whole thing</u> again using <u>different masses</u> to give different <u>forces</u>.
10) You should find the <u>greater</u> the <u>force</u> (more masses), the <u>greater</u> the <u>acceleration</u>.
11) You could also <u>change the mass of the trolley</u> to show that the <u>bigger</u> the <u>mass</u> of the <u>object</u>, the <u>smaller</u> the <u>acceleration</u>.

Investigating acceleration — you've got to be off your trolley...

So, a resultant force makes an object accelerate. $\underline{F = m \times a}$ is bound to crop up in the exam — so learn it good.

__Revision Summary for P2a Topics 1, 2 & 3__

Here are some jolly questions which I know you're going to enjoy. You know what to do with the tricky ones — read over the right stuff again, then have another go at them. Keep at it until you can do every question.

1) Draw and label a sketch to show the structure of an atom.

2) What causes the build-up of static electricity? Which particles move when static builds up?

3) Explain why a negatively charged comb is able to pick up little pieces of uncharged paper.

4) Describe how electrostatic paint sprayers use static electricity to get an even coat of paint.

5) Explain how you can reduce the danger of getting a static electric shock.

6) Give the definition for current.

7) What type of current do cells and batteries supply?

8) In a circuit, what happens if you increase: a) potential difference?   b) resistance?

9) Should a voltmeter be placed in series or in parallel with a component in a circuit?

10) Sketch a typical graph of current (I) against potential difference (V) for:
a) a fixed resistor,   b) a filament lamp,   c) a diode.

11) Describe how the resistance of an LDR changes with light intensity.

$P = I \times V$

12) Resistors get hot when an electric current passes through them.
Describe three advantages of this.

13)* Calculate the power of a toaster that uses a voltage of 230 V and has a current of 4.8 A flowing through it.

14) What's the difference between speed and velocity?

15)* Find the speed of a partly chewed mouse which hobbles 3.5 m in 35 s. $s = d \div t$

16) What is acceleration? What is the unit used?

17)* Find the acceleration of a soggy pea flicked from rest to a speed of 14 m/s in 0.4 seconds.

18) Sketch a typical distance-time graph and point out all the important parts of it.

$a = \dfrac{(v - u)}{t}$

19) Sketch a typical velocity-time graph and point out all the important parts.

20) Sketch two standard force diagrams, showing the forces and the types of motion.

21) What is "terminal velocity"?

22) Explain what a reaction force is and where it pops up.

23) If an object has zero resultant force on it, can it be moving? Can it be accelerating?

24)* Find the resultant force of a ball of mass 2 kg accelerating at 5 m/s². $F = m \times a$

Stopping Distances

The stopping distance of a car is the distance it travels in the time between the driver <u>first spotting</u> a hazard (danger) and the car coming to a <u>complete stop</u>.

Many Things Affect Your Total Stopping Distance

The distance it takes to stop a car is made up of the <u>total</u> of the <u>THINKING DISTANCE</u> and the <u>BRAKING DISTANCE</u>.

1) Thinking Distance

"The distance the car travels in the time between the driver spotting a hazard and hitting the brakes."

It's affected by <u>TWO MAIN FACTORS</u>:

a) Your REACTION time — <u>Tiredness</u>, <u>drugs</u>, <u>alcohol</u>, <u>old age</u> and a <u>careless</u> attitude can <u>increase</u> the time it takes for you to <u>react</u> to a <u>hazard</u>.

b) How FAST you're going — the <u>faster</u> you're going, the <u>further</u> you'll go.

2) Braking Distance

"The distance the car travels under the braking force (i.e. while braking)."

It's affected by <u>FOUR MAIN FACTORS</u>:

a) How FAST you're going — the <u>faster</u> you're going, the <u>further</u> it takes to stop.

b) The MASS of your vehicle — with the <u>same</u> brakes, a <u>heavy</u> vehicle takes <u>longer to stop</u>.

c) How good your BRAKES are — Worn or faulty brakes will <u>let you down</u> just when you need them the <u>most</u>, i.e. in an <u>emergency</u>.

d) How good the GRIP is — you need <u>friction</u> between your <u>tyres</u> and the <u>road surface</u> to be able to <u>stop</u>. This depends on: 1) <u>road surface</u>, 2) <u>weather</u> conditions, 3) <u>tyres</u>.

Wet or icy roads are always much more slippy than dry roads because there isn't much friction between the tyres and the road.

Different Surfaces Provide Different Amounts of Friction

1) We can see how the <u>amount of force</u> needed to <u>slide a block</u> changes with <u>different surfaces</u> by using the experiment below.

2) Set up your <u>apparatus</u> as shown here:

3) Add <u>masses</u> one by one to the <u>mass holder</u>.

4) This applies a <u>force</u> to the block until it <u>slides</u>.

5) The <u>amount</u> of force (the amount of mass) needed to slide the block will depend on the amount of <u>friction</u> between the <u>block</u> and the <u>surface</u>.

6) This is just like the <u>tyres</u> of a vehicle driving on different <u>road surfaces</u>.

7) The <u>smaller</u> the frictional force between the block and the surface, the <u>smaller</u> the force you'll need to make the block slide.

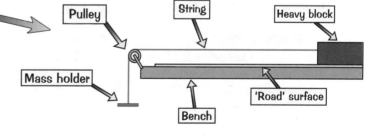

Pulley | String | Heavy block | Mass holder | Bench | 'Road' surface

You can experiment with different surfaces — try foil, sandpaper, plastic covered in washing up liquid...

Stop right there — and learn this page...

Scary stuff. Learn all the different things that affect thinking and braking distance, they're well important.

Car Safety

A large lorry being driven very fast is going to be a lot harder to stop than a granny on a bicycle out for a Sunday afternoon ride — that's momentum for you.

Momentum = Mass × Velocity

1) All moving objects have momentum. The momentum of an object depends on its mass and velocity:

$$\text{Momentum (kg m/s)} = \text{Mass (kg)} \times \text{Velocity (m/s)}$$

2) The greater the mass of an object and the greater its velocity, the more momentum the object has.

3) Momentum is a vector quantity — it has size (magnitude) and direction.

Momentum Before = Momentum After

1) In collisions and explosions, momentum is conserved.

2) This means that the total momentum after is the same as it was before.

Example:

Two skaters approach each other, collide and move off together as shown. What is their total momentum after the collision?

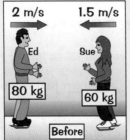

1) Choose which direction is positive. I'll say "positive" means "to the right". So Ed's velocity will be +2 m/s and Sue's will be –1.5 m/s.

2) Total momentum before collision
= momentum of Ed + momentum of Sue
= {80 × 2} + {60 × (–1.5)} = 70 kg m/s

3) Total momentum after = Total momentum before
= 70 kg m/s

Forces Cause Changes in Momentum

1) When a force acts on an object, it causes a change in momentum.

2) If someone's momentum changes very quickly (like in a car crash), the forces on the body will be very large, and more likely to cause injury.

3) The longer it takes for a change in momentum, the smaller the force.

4) This is why cars are designed with protective features (see below) to slow people down over a longer time when they have a crash.

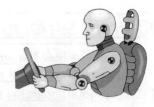

> CRUMPLE ZONES crumple on impact. This increases the time taken for the car to stop, so reduces the force of the crash.

> SEAT BELTS stretch slightly, increasing the time taken for the wearer to stop. This reduces the forces acting on the chest.

> AIR BAGS also slow the passengers down more slowly and so reduces the forces on them.

5) Bubble wrap works in a similar way to crumple zones. It increases the time over which any knocks happen to the stuff inside it — reducing the forces on them.

6) The effect of crumple zones can be shown using eggs.
   - Drop an egg on a hard floor and the force of the impact will cause it to break.
   - If you build it a crumple zone, e.g. out of bubble wrap, it might not break when you drop it.
   - The bubble wrap increases the time taken for the egg to stop, and so the force on the egg is smaller.

Learn this stuff — it'll only take a moment... um...

Momentum's a pretty important bit of Physics. Remember, the longer a change in momentum takes, the smaller the force. Who'd have thought bubble wrap could be so interesting... And so much fun to pop.

Work and Power

Work work work. I bet you're sick of work, but I tell you what — read this page and maybe you'll learn to love it.

Work is Done When a Force Moves an Object

When a force moves an object, energy is transferred and work is done.

1) Whenever something moves, something else is putting in some sort of 'effort' to move it.

2) The thing putting the effort in needs a supply of energy (like fuel or food or electricity etc.).

3) It then does 'work' by moving the object — it transfers the energy it receives (as fuel etc.) into other forms.

4) Energy transferred is equal to work done. Both are measured in joules, J.

5) The amount of work done on an object depends on the distance that the force moves the object.

6) Work done is given by this formula:

Work Done = Force × Distance moved in the direction of the force

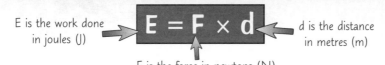

E is the work done in joules (J)

$$E = F \times d$$

d is the distance in metres (m)

F is the force in newtons (N)

EXAMPLE: Some kids drag a tractor tyre 5 m. They pull with a total force of 340 N. Find the energy transferred.

ANSWER: Energy transferred is work done, so: $E = F \times d = 340 \text{ N} \times 5 \text{ m} = \underline{1700 \text{ J}}$.

Power is the "Rate of Doing Work" — How Much per Second

1) Power is not the same thing as force, and it's not the same thing as energy.

2) Power is the rate of doing work.

3) This just means how much energy can be transferred per second.

4) The proper unit of power is the watt (W).

5) One watt = 1 joule of energy transferred per second (J/s).

6) This is the formula for power:

7) A powerful machine is one that transfers a lot of energy in a short space of time.

$$\text{Power (W)} = \frac{\text{Work done (J)}}{\text{Time taken (s)}} \qquad P = \frac{E}{t}$$

EXAMPLE: A motor transfers 4800 J of useful energy in 2 minutes. Find its power output.

ANSWER: First, convert minutes to seconds: $t = 2 \text{ mins} = (2 \times 60) = 120 \text{ s}$.
$P = E \div t = 4800 \text{ J} \div 120 \text{ s} = \underline{40 \text{ W}}$ (or 40 J/s)

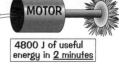

4800 J of useful energy in 2 minutes

Force yourself to do some work and learn this page...

Whenever you move an object a distance you do work — even if it's just rolling a pencil along your desk. Don't get confused by work done and energy transferred — like Spider-Man and Peter Parker they're one and the same.

Kinetic and Potential Energy

Sat <u>high</u> on your stool in science class you have <u>gravitational potential energy</u> — there's always the potential to fall backwards off it and look a <u>right tool</u>. So be careful — studying's a risky business...

Kinetic Energy *is Energy of* Movement

1) Anything that's <u>moving</u> has <u>kinetic energy</u> (K.E.).

2) The <u>kinetic energy</u> of something depends both on its <u>mass</u> and <u>velocity</u>.

3) The <u>heavier it is</u> and the <u>faster it's going</u>, the <u>bigger</u> its kinetic energy will be.

4) There's a slightly <u>tricky formula</u> for it:

In this formula, K.E. is in J, mass is in kg and v is in m/s.

$$\text{Kinetic Energy} = \tfrac{1}{2} \times \text{mass} \times \text{velocity}^2$$

$$\text{K.E.} = \tfrac{1}{2} \times m \times v^2$$

<u>EXAMPLE:</u> A car of mass 2450 kg is travelling at 38 m/s. Calculate its kinetic energy.

<u>ANSWER:</u> Plug the numbers into the formula — but watch the 'v²'!

K.E. $= \tfrac{1}{2} \times m \times v^2 = \tfrac{1}{2} \times 2450 \times 38^2 = \underline{1\,768\,900}$ J. (<u>Joules</u> because it's <u>energy</u>.)

small mass, not fast
low kinetic energy

big fast
lorries Ltd

big mass, real fast
high kinetic energy

Gravitational Potential Energy *is Energy* Due to Height

1) When you lift an object up it gains <u>gravitational potential energy</u> (G.P.E)

2) The gravitational potential energy of an object depends on its <u>mass</u>, the gravitational field strength, <u>g</u>, and the <u>height</u> it is lifted to.

3) The units for g are <u>newtons per kilogram</u> (N/kg).

4) On <u>Earth</u>, g is approximately <u>10 N/kg</u>.

See p. 87 for more on g.

In this formula, G.P.E. is in J, mass is in kg, g is in N/kg and h is in m.

$$\text{Gravitational Potential Energy} = \text{mass} \times g \times \text{height}$$

$$\text{G.P.E.} = m \times g \times h$$

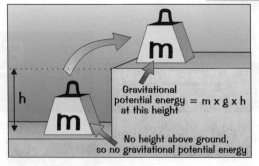

Gravitational potential energy = m x g x h at this height

No height above ground, so no gravitational potential energy

<u>EXAMPLE:</u> A sheep of mass 47 kg is lifted 6.3 m. Find the gain in gravitational potential energy.

<u>ANSWER:</u> G.P.E. $= m \times g \times h = 47 \times 10 \times 6.3 = \underline{2961}$ J. (<u>Joules</u> because it's <u>energy</u>.)

I could fall for you — if I had gravitational potential energy...

On Earth, the <u>gravitational field strength</u> is around <u>10 N/kg</u>, which is really handy because it makes calculations for G.P.E. easier. As for calculating K.E., that's a bit trickier, which means you have to practise lots. Soz.

Conservation of Energy

What goes up must come down — that's the principle of the conservation of energy in action.

The Principle of the Conservation of Energy is this:

> Energy can never be created nor destroyed
> — only converted (changed) from one form to another.

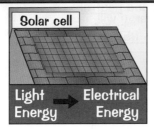

Solar cell

Light Energy → Electrical Energy

falling object

Gravitational Potential Energy → Kinetic Energy

Falling Objects Convert G.P.E. to K.E.

1) When something falls, its gravitational potential energy is converted into kinetic energy.

2) In the real world, some of the G.P.E. will be transferred to heat due to air resistance.

3) But most of the time you can ignore that and learn this equation instead:

> Kinetic energy gained = Gravitational potential energy lost

G.P.E.
↓
K.E.

> EXAMPLE: A tomato of mass 0.14 kg is dropped from a height of 1.7 m.
> Calculate its kinetic energy just before it hits the floor.
>
> ANSWER: Find G.P.E. lost: G.P.E. = m × g × h, m = 0.14 kg, g = 10 N/kg, h = 1.7m
> m × g × h = 0.14 × 10 × 1.7 = 2.38 J
> K.E. gained = G.P.E. lost, so K.E. = 2.38 J.

Most Energy Transfers Involve Some Wasted Energy, Often as Heat

1) Every time energy is transferred from one form to another, some of the energy is wasted.

2) Often this energy is wasted as heat, and sometimes as sound.

3) For example, in a car you want all the chemical energy of the fuel to be transferred into kinetic energy.

4) But the car warms up and makes a load of noise, so some energy is wasted as heat and sound.

5) The Principle of the Conservation of Energy says the total amount of energy stays the same.

6) So the energy is still there, but it can't be easily used or collected back in again.

Conserve your energy — you'll need it for the next page...

Make sure you're happy with converting gravitational potential energy to kinetic energy — it's one of those ideas that pops up in exams time and time again. Cover the answer to the example above and have a go at it now.

Radioactivity

First up, a <u>clever way</u> of writing the number of protons and neutrons in an atom...

Elements *can be Described Using Atomic and Mass Numbers*

1) The <u>nucleus</u> of an atom (p.76) contains <u>protons</u> and <u>neutrons</u>.

2) Different <u>elements</u> have different <u>numbers</u> of protons in their nucleus.

3) We can <u>describe</u> different elements like <u>this</u>:

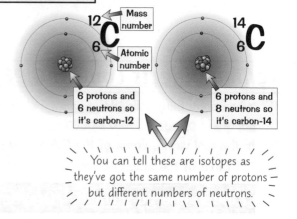

EXAMPLE: OXYGEN

THE MASS (NUCLEON) NUMBER → ^{16}
= total number of <u>protons</u> and <u>neutrons</u>

THE ATOMIC (PROTON) NUMBER → $_{8}$O
= number of <u>protons</u>

O is the chemical symbol for oxygen.

Isotopes *are Different Forms of the Same Element*

1) <u>Isotopes</u> are atoms with the <u>same</u> number of <u>protons</u> in their nucleus, but a <u>different</u> number of <u>neutrons</u>.

2) This means they have the <u>same atomic number</u>, but <u>different mass numbers</u>.

3) For example, <u>carbon-12</u> and <u>carbon-14</u> are both isotopes of carbon:

4) Some isotopes are <u>unstable</u> and <u>radioactive</u>.

5) This means they <u>decay</u> (break down) into <u>other elements</u> and <u>give out energy as radiation</u>.

$^{12}_{6}$C   Mass number   Atomic number

6 protons and 6 neutrons so it's carbon-12

$^{14}_{6}$C

6 protons and 8 neutrons so it's carbon-14

You can tell these are isotopes as they've got the same number of protons but different numbers of neutrons.

We Can't Predict When *an Unstable Nucleus* will Decay

1) <u>Unstable nuclei</u> will <u>decay</u> and <u>give out ionising radiation</u> (see below).

2) This decay is <u>random</u> — you can't predict (say) when it will happen.

3) When the nucleus <u>does</u> decay it will <u>emit</u> (give out) one or more of three types of radiation — <u>alpha</u>, <u>beta</u> or <u>gamma</u>.

Alpha, Beta *and Gamma Radiation can Cause Ionisation*

1) Atoms can <u>gain</u> or <u>lose electrons</u>.

2) When an atom loses or gains an electron it is turned into an <u>ion</u>. This is called <u>ionisation</u>.

3) <u>Alpha</u>, <u>beta</u> and <u>gamma</u> are all types of <u>ionising radiation</u> — they can cause <u>ionisation</u> of atoms.

4) <u>Alpha particles</u> are <u>positively</u> charged. When an alpha particle passes <u>close</u> to an atom, it can <u>pull</u> a <u>negatively-charged</u> electron away from the atom.

5) <u>Beta particles</u> are negatively charged. They can <u>push</u> electrons away from their atoms (remember that like charges <u>repel</u> each other).

6) <u>Gamma rays</u> can <u>transfer energy</u> to electrons. If the electron gets <u>enough energy</u>, it can <u>break free</u> from the atom.

See the next page for info on <u>how well</u> alpha, beta and gamma ionise.

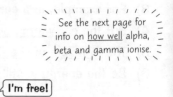

I'm free!

Completely random — *just like your revision shouldn't be...*

Only <u>unstable isotopes</u> go through <u>radioactive decay</u> and give out <u>radiation</u> — which can be either alpha, beta or gamma. There's lots more to know about those three — the next page is packed full of fun facts all about them.

Radioactivity

What's that? You want to hear more about <u>alpha</u>, <u>beta</u> and <u>gamma radiation</u>? Well, since you asked nicely...

Alpha, Beta *and* Gamma Radiation *Have* Different Properties

You need to remember <u>three things</u> about <u>alpha</u>, <u>beta</u> and <u>gamma radiation</u>:

1) What it <u>actually is</u>.

2) How strongly it <u>ionises</u> a material (how easily it removes electrons from atoms — see page 96).

3) How well it <u>penetrates</u> (travels through) materials.

Alpha Particles *are* Helium Nuclei $^4_2$He

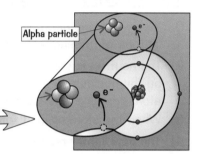

1) Alpha particles are made up of <u>two protons</u> and <u>two neutrons</u>.

2) Compared to beta and gamma, they are <u>big</u> and <u>heavy</u> and <u>slow-moving</u>.

3) They have a <u>strong positive charge</u>.

4) They are <u>strongly ionising</u>. This means they can remove electrons from lots of atoms, making lots of ions.

5) They <u>don't penetrate</u> far into materials — they're <u>stopped quickly</u>.

Beta Particles *are* Electrons Emitted *from a* Nucleus 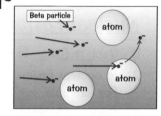 $^0_{-1}$e

1) Beta particles are electrons so they move <u>quite fast</u> and are <u>quite small</u>.

2) They have a <u>negative charge</u>.

3) They are <u>fairly ionising</u>.

4) They <u>penetrate quite far</u> into materials before being <u>stopped</u> — they travel further than alpha particles.

Gamma Rays *are a Type of* Electromagnetic Radiation

1) Gamma rays are high energy waves from the <u>electromagnetic spectrum</u>.

2) They are <u>weakly ionising</u>.

3) They <u>penetrate a long way</u> into materials.

The Three Types *of* Radiation *can be* Blocked...

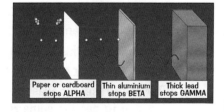

1) <u>Alpha particles</u> are blocked by <u>paper</u> and <u>cardboard</u>.

2) <u>Beta particles</u> are blocked by thin <u>aluminium</u>.

3) <u>Gamma rays</u> are blocked by <u>thick lead</u>.

Don't block this information out — let it penetrate your mind...

Three things to learn for each ionising radiation type — what it is, how ionising it is and how well it penetrates stuff. The different <u>properties</u> of each radiation makes them useful for <u>different jobs</u> — but you'll find out about that later.

Nuclear Fission and Fusion

Loads of energy's released either when you break apart <u>really big atoms</u> or join together <u>really small ones</u>.

Nuclear Fission — The Splitting Up of Big Atoms

1) <u>Nuclear fission</u> is a type of <u>nuclear reaction</u> that is used to <u>release energy</u> from <u>big atoms</u> (such as uranium or plutonium).

2) This happens when the <u>nucleus</u> of a <u>big atom</u> splits into the <u>nuclei</u> of <u>smaller atoms</u>.

3) In a <u>nuclear power station</u>, <u>huge amounts</u> of energy can be released by using a nuclear fission <u>chain reaction</u>.

The Chain Reaction:

1) A <u>slow-moving neutron</u> is fired at an isotope of uranium — uranium-235.

2) The neutron is <u>absorbed</u> (taken in) by the nucleus — this makes the atom <u>unstable</u> and causes it to split.

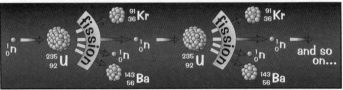

A nuclear fission chain reaction in a nuclear reactor.

3) When the atom splits it forms <u>two new lighter</u> elements ('<u>daughter nuclei</u>') and <u>energy</u> is released.

4) The new lighter nuclei are <u>radioactive</u> (see p.96).

5) Each time a <u>uranium</u> atom <u>splits up</u>, it also spits out <u>two or three neutrons</u>.

6) These neutrons can hit <u>other</u> uranium nuclei, causing them to <u>split</u> too, and so on. This is a <u>chain reaction</u>.

Nuclear Fusion — The Joining of Small Nuclei

1) <u>Nuclear fusion</u> is the <u>opposite</u> of nuclear fission.

2) In nuclear fusion, two <u>light nuclei</u> fuse (join) to create a <u>larger</u> nucleus. For example, <u>hydrogen</u> nuclei can fuse to produce <u>helium nuclei</u>.

3) Fusion releases <u>a lot</u> of <u>energy</u> — <u>more than fission</u> for the same amount of fuel.

4) All the energy released in <u>stars</u> comes from fusion.

5) Unlike nuclear fission, nuclear fusion <u>doesn't</u> leave behind a lot of radioactive <u>waste</u>. And there's <u>plenty</u> of hydrogen around to use as <u>fuel</u>.

6) But at the moment, scientists can't create the <u>right conditions</u> for fusion to make <u>more energy</u> than it uses.

Cold Fusion — Energy of the Future?

1) Cold fusion is <u>nuclear fusion</u> that happens at <u>room temperature</u>.

2) In 1989 two scientists reported that they had released energy from <u>cold fusion</u>.

3) This caused a lot of <u>excitement</u> because cold fusion could generate lots of electricity.

4) However, the theory of cold fusion <u>hasn't been accepted by scientists</u>.

5) One reason for this is that their cold fusion research wasn't <u>peer reviewed</u> before it was reported. This means <u>other scientists</u> hadn't looked at their work to check it was <u>reliable</u>.

6) After their research was reported, other scientists tried to repeat the work, but <u>only a few</u> managed to get the <u>same results reliably</u> (get the same results again and again).

Pity they can't release energy by confusion...*

Getting a scientific theory accepted can <u>take ages</u> — it has to be sent to <u>lots of different scientists</u> so that they can check that the experiment works. If the other scientists gets the same results, the theory gets accepted.

*There'd be plenty of physics books to use as fuel.

Nuclear Power Stations

It's amazing how much <u>energy</u> there is <u>trapped</u> in a tiny atom — and we can use it to generate electricity.

Nuclear Power Stations <u>are Powered by</u> <u>Nuclear Reactors</u>

See below for how a chain reaction is controlled.

1) In a nuclear reactor, a <u>controlled chain reaction</u> of nuclear fission takes place.

2) The <u>heat energy</u> released by nuclear fission is used to <u>boil water</u> to drive a <u>steam turbine</u>.

3) This turns a <u>generator</u> to generate <u>electrical energy</u>.

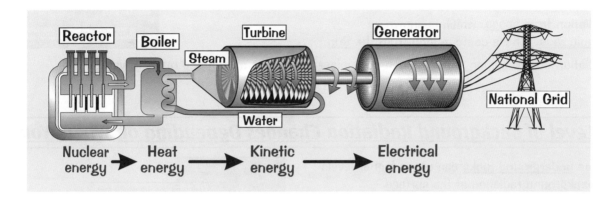

Chain Reactions <u>in Reactors Must be</u> <u>Carefully Controlled</u>

1) The <u>neutrons</u> released by fission in a nuclear reactor have <u>a lot</u> of energy.

2) These neutrons will only cause <u>other</u> nuclear fissions if they are <u>moving slow</u> enough to be <u>captured</u> (caught) by the uranium nuclei in the fuel rods.

3) The uranium <u>fuel rods</u> are put in a <u>moderator</u> (e.g. water or graphite) to <u>slow down</u> the fast moving neutrons.

4) <u>Control rods</u> are placed <u>in between</u> the fuel rods.

5) They are <u>raised</u> and <u>lowered</u> into the reactor to <u>control</u> the chain reaction.

6) The <u>control rods</u> are used to <u>absorb neutrons</u> so that the chain reaction can be <u>slowed down</u>.

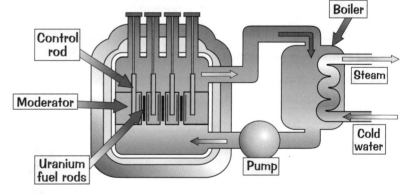

7) This creates a <u>steady rate</u> of nuclear fission, where <u>one new neutron</u> produces another fission.

8) If the chain reaction in a nuclear reactor <u>isn't controlled</u>, large amounts of <u>energy</u> are <u>released</u> in a very <u>short time</u>, which could lead to an <u>explosion</u>.

Revise nuclear power — full steam ahead...

When nuclear fission is used to produce energy in power stations, the chain reaction has to be <u>controlled</u> so that <u>safe</u> amounts of energy are released. More of a problem is the <u>radioactive waste</u> that's produced (see p. 104).

Background Radiation and Half-life

There's radiation all around us, all the time. But don't panic — it won't hurt, honest.

Background Radiation Comes from Many Sources

Background radiation is the low-level radiation that's around us all the time. Background radiation comes from:

1) The decay of natural unstable isotopes (see p.96) which are all around us. For example, they're in the air, in food, in building materials and in the rocks under our feet.

2) Radiation from space, which is known as cosmic rays. These come mostly from the Sun.

3) Radiation due to human activity, such as nuclear explosions or dumped nuclear waste.

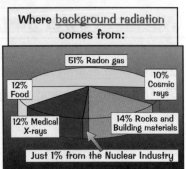

Where background radiation comes from:

51% Radon gas
10% Cosmic rays
12% Food
12% Medical X-rays
14% Rocks and Building materials
Just 1% from the Nuclear Industry

The Level of Background Radiation Changes Depending on Where You Are

1) Some underground rocks can cause higher levels of background radiation at the surface.

2) Some rocks release radioactive radon gas, which can get trapped inside people's houses.

3) The amount of background radiation from radon in people's houses changes across the UK. It depends on the type of rock the house is built on.

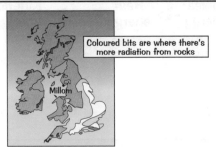

Coloured bits are where there's more radiation from rocks

Millom

The Activity of a Source Always Decreases Over Time

1) Radiation is given out when a nucleus decays. How often this happens is called the activity.

2) The activity of a radioactive source always decreases (gets less) over time.

3) Each time a radioactive nucleus decays (see page 96) one more radioactive nucleus disappears.

4) As more and more unstable nuclei decay, there will be fewer left to decay.

5) So the older a source becomes, the less radiation it will emit — its activity decreases.

6) For some isotopes it takes just a few hours before nearly all the unstable nuclei have decayed, whilst others last for millions of years.

7) But the activity of a radioactive source never reaches zero.

8) So we use the idea of half-life to measure how quickly the activity falls.

The **HALF-LIFE** of a radioactive isotope is the **TIME TAKEN** for **HALF** of the undecayed nuclei to **DECAY**.

9) A short half-life means the activity falls quickly, because lots of the nuclei decay quickly.

10) A long half-life means the activity falls more slowly because most of the nuclei don't decay for a long time.

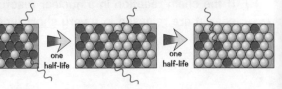

one half-life   one half-life

11) The activity of a radioactive isotope is measured in becquerels (Bq). 1 Bq is 1 decay per second.

Background radiation — the ugly wallpaper of the Universe...

Background radiation was found by accident. Scientists were measuring the radioactivity of materials, but they detected radioactivity when there was no material being tested. They realised it was natural background radiation.

Calculating Half-life

Half-life is a tricky topic. We can work out the half-life of a sample by looking at its activity over time.

Calculating Half-Life is Best Done Step by Step

EXAMPLE: The activity of a radioactive isotope is 640 Bq.
Two hours later it has fallen to 40 Bq. Find the half-life of the sample.

ANSWER: Go through it in short simple steps like this:

INITIAL (starting) count:		after ONE half-life:		after TWO half-lives:		after THREE half-lives:		after FOUR half-lives:
640	(÷2) →	320	(÷2) →	160	(÷2) →	80	(÷2) →	40

So, it takes four half-lives for the activity to fall from 640 to 40.
Two hours must be four half-lives: 2 ÷ 4 = 0.5, so the half-life is 0.5 hours (30 minutes).

Measuring the Half-Life of a Source Using a Graph

1) The activity of a radioactive source can be plotted against time as a graph.

2) Background radiation can affect readings. So the background activity of the source is measured first and then taken away from every reading, before the results are plotted on the graph.

3) The half-life can then be found from the graph.

4) First, read the initial activity on the vertical (↑) axis (on this graph it is 800 Bq).

5) Halve this activity (here to 400 Bq) and draw a horizontal (→) line across to the graph.

6) Draw a line straight down, and the line that hits the bottom axis tells you the time it took for the activity to halve — this is the half-life.

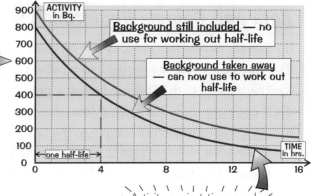

Background still included — no use for working out half-life

Background taken away — can now use to work out half-life

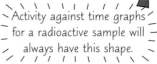

Activity against time graphs for a radioactive sample will always have this shape.

You Can Use Models to Simulate Radioactive Decay

1) The radioactive dice model is one way of simulating (modelling) the radioactive decay of a sample:

2) 24 dice represent 24 atoms of an unstable isotope that could decay at any moment.

3) The dice are rolled together — this represents one unit of time. All the dice that come up with a six are said to have 'decayed' and are removed.

4) The dice that are left are the undecayed atoms.

5) The dice are rolled again and again and the results are plotted on a graph with a best fit curve.

6) You can use the graph to find the half life of the sample (see above).

7) This is like radioactive decay because it's completely random which dice will come up with a six on each roll.

8) The shape of the graph is the same as one you would get from the activity of a radioactive source.

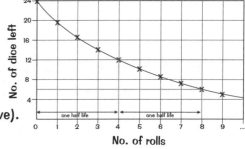

Half-life of a box of chocolates — about five minutes...

Go through that example at the top of the page nice and slowly and do loads of practice. You'll be glad you did.

Uses of Radioactivity

Some clever scientists thought up <u>uses</u> for all that radioactivity — and now you get to learn about 'em, hurrah.

Household Fire Alarms — Use Alpha Radiation

1) A <u>weak</u> source of alpha radiation is placed in a smoke detector.
2) The source causes <u>ionisation</u> of the air — which causes a <u>current</u> to flow.
3) If there is a fire then smoke will <u>absorb</u> the radiation — the current stops and the <u>alarm sounds</u>.

Sterilisation of Food and Equipment Using Gamma Rays

1) <u>Food</u> can be <u>irradiated with</u> (exposed to) a <u>high dose</u> of <u>gamma rays</u>.
2) This will <u>kill</u> all <u>microbes</u> (germs) so that the food doesn't go bad as quickly. We say that the food has been <u>sterilised</u>.
3) <u>Medical equipment</u> can also be <u>sterilised</u> using gamma rays.

Beta and Gamma Radiation are Used in Tracers

Medical tracers should have a short half-life so that the radioactivity inside the patient quickly disappears.

1) Certain radioactive isotopes can be used as <u>tracers</u>.
2) A <u>medical</u> tracer is <u>injected</u> into a patient (or <u>swallowed</u>) and travels around the body.
3) The tracer's path is followed using a <u>detector</u> outside the body.
4) A <u>computer</u> uses the reading from the detector to <u>spot</u> and <u>diagnose medical conditions</u> (such as <u>cancer</u>).
5) <u>All isotopes</u> which are taken <u>into the body</u> must be <u>BETA or GAMMA</u> emitters (never alpha), so that the radiation <u>passes out of the body</u> (see next page).
6) <u>Gamma emitting tracers</u> are also used in <u>industry</u> to detect <u>leaks</u> in <u>underground pipes</u>.

Beta Radiation Can be Used to Control Thickness

1) When making something like paper, radiation is sent through it to a <u>detector</u> on the other side.
2) When the amount of radiation detected <u>changes</u>, it means the paper is coming out <u>too thick</u> or <u>too thin</u>.
3) So the <u>rollers move</u> to correct the thickness.
4) <u>Beta</u> radiation is used in thickness gauges because it will get <u>partially blocked</u> by thicker paper.

Gamma Rays Can Be Used to Treat Cancer

1) High doses of gamma rays will <u>kill all living cells</u> (see next page).
2) For this reason, they can be used to <u>treat cancers</u>.
3) Hospital workers have to be very careful when treating a patient to <u>direct</u> the gamma rays right at the <u>cancerous</u> cells.
4) They do this to try and <u>reduce</u> the damage done to <u>healthy</u> cells.

Ionising radiation — just what the doctor ordered...

Radiation has many important uses especially in <u>medicine</u>. Examiners just love to ask you questions on this stuff.

Dangers of Radioactivity

Ionising Radiation Can Cause Tissue Damage and Cell Mutation

1) Alpha, beta and gamma radiation will enter living cells and collide with molecules.

2) These collisions cause ionisation (see p. 96), which leads to tissue damage.

3) Lower doses can create mutant cells which multiply. This is cancer.

4) Higher doses can kill cells — which causes radiation sickness.

5) How harmful the radiation is depends on two things:

    a) How much exposure you have to the radiation.

    b) The energy and penetration of the radiation (see p. 97).

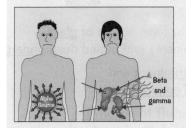

1) Outside the body, beta and gamma sources are the most dangerous.

2) This is because beta and gamma can get inside to the organs.

3) Alpha is less dangerous outside the body because it can't get through the skin.

4) Inside the body, an alpha source is the most dangerous.

5) Beta and gamma mostly pass straight out without doing much damage.

Attitudes Towards the Dangers of Radioactivity have Changed

1) When Marie Curie discovered radioactive radium in 1898, nobody knew anything about its dangers.

2) It was used in medicines and to make luminous paint, e.g. for glow-in-the-dark watches.

3) But by the 1930s people were starting to link health problems to radiation. Many watch dial painters developed cancer and died as a result of exposure to radium.

4) We've learnt about some of the long-term effects of radiation from events like the Chernobyl disaster.

5) We now know it is important to take precautions when working with radioactive sources.

You Should Protect Yourself in the Laboratory...

1) You should be exposed to radioactive sources for the shortest amount of time possible.

2) Never allow skin contact with a source. Always handle sources with tongs.

3) Keep the source at arm's length to keep it as far from the body as possible.

4) Keep the source pointing away from the body and avoid looking directly at it.

5) Put the source back in a labelled lead box when the experiment is over, to keep your exposure time short.

...and If You Work with Nuclear Radiation

1) Industrial nuclear workers wear protective suits to stop them touching or breathing in radioactive particles.

2) Lead-lined suits, lead/concrete barriers and thick lead screens are used to stop exposure to gamma rays.

3) Workers use remote-controlled robot arms to carry out tasks in highly radioactive areas.

Revision sickness — never mind, it'll wear off...

Scientists can't do radiation research on humans because it would be unethical. What we know about how radiation affects people comes from studies of populations affected by nuclear accidents or nuclear bombs.

Nuclear Power

Nuclear power is one seriously awesome power source. It's a pity that it creates so much radioactive waste :(

Nuclear Waste is a Big Problem for the Nuclear Industry

1) <u>Nuclear fission</u> releases a <u>lot of energy</u> that can be used to <u>generate electricity</u> (see page 99).

2) But it also creates <u>radioactive waste</u> that can't just be <u>thrown away</u>.

3) Radioactive waste can have a <u>very long half-life</u>.
This means it will be <u>radioactive</u> for <u>hundreds</u> or even <u>thousands</u> of <u>years</u>.

4) Radioactive waste needs to be put somewhere <u>far away</u>
from <u>people</u> to stop it causing any <u>harm</u> (see previous page).

5) Nuclear power stations usually deal with the
<u>most dangerous</u> nuclear waste by <u>vitrification</u>.

6) This means they <u>melt</u> the waste with other materials to form a type of <u>glass</u>.
The liquid glass is sealed inside <u>steel canisters</u> (containers) and buried deep <u>underground</u>.

7) Nuclear waste can also be packed into <u>thick metal containers</u> and
buried in a deep hole which is then filled with <u>tons of concrete</u>.

8) It's buried deep underground so that there's a lot of stuff to <u>absorb the
radiation</u> from nuclear waste before it can reach the surface of the Earth.

Using Nuclear Power Has Its Pros and Cons

1) Lots of people think that generating electricity by using nuclear power is <u>very dangerous</u>.

2) Some people worry that nuclear <u>waste</u> (see above) could <u>leak out</u> and <u>pollute</u> land, rivers and oceans.

3) There have been <u>accidents</u> that have covered <u>huge areas</u> with radioactive material.
Some people think the energy generated by nuclear power is <u>not worth the risk</u> of nuclear accidents.

4) However, nuclear power is generally a <u>pretty safe</u> way of generating
electricity — it's not as <u>risky</u> as <u>some people may think</u> it is.

5) Nuclear power is a <u>very reliable</u> energy resource.

6) It reduces the need for <u>fossil fuels</u> (which are already starting to run out).

7) Nuclear power <u>doesn't</u> release <u>carbon dioxide</u> (CO_2) like <u>fossil fuels</u> do.
So in this way it is a very <u>clean</u> source of energy.

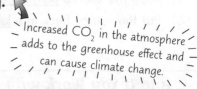

Increased CO_2 in the atmosphere adds to the greenhouse effect and can cause climate change.

8) <u>Nuclear fuel</u> is <u>cheap</u> and <u>available</u>. It can also generate a <u>lot of energy</u>.

9) But the <u>overall cost</u> of nuclear power is <u>high</u>.
This is because it is very expensive to <u>set up</u> a power plant, and
<u>decommissioning</u> (taking apart) one <u>safely</u> takes <u>decades</u>.

Eating radioactive sheep? That's probably bad for ewe...

In 1986 the <u>Chernobyl</u> nuclear power plant in Ukraine exploded and released loads of <u>nuclear radiation</u> into the
surrounding area. Nearby cities had to be totally evacuated. Today, the areas around Chernobyl <u>remain deserted</u>.

Revision Summary for P2b Topics 4, 5 & 6

Right, you've conquered three more revision topics — time to see if any of it has stuck. Good luck chaps.

1) What are the two different parts of the overall stopping distance of a car?

2) List two factors which affect each of the two parts of the stopping distance.

3)* Find the momentum of a 78 kg sheep falling at 15 m/s.

momentum = mass × velocity

4) Explain how seat belts, crumple zones and air bags are useful in a car crash.

5)* A crazy dog drags a big branch 12 m over the next-door neighbour's front lawn, pulling with a force of 535 N. How much energy is transferred?

E = F × d

K.E. = ½ × m × v²

6) What are the units of power?

7)* Find the kinetic energy of a 78 kg sheep moving at 23 m/s.

8)* Calculate the increase in gravitational potential energy when a box of mass 12 kg is lifted through 4.5 m. (Assume g = 10 N/kg.)

9)* Assuming no air resistance, calculate the kinetic energy of a 78 kg sheep just as it hits the floor after falling from a height of 20 m.

G.P.E = m × g × h

10) Explain what the mass number and atomic number of an atom represent.

11) Explain what isotopes are. Do stable or unstable isotopes undergo nuclear decay?

12) Describe the properties of the three types of radiation:
a) alpha, b) beta, c) gamma.

13) Name a substance that will block each of the three types of radiation.

14) Describe the chain reaction that's started by firing a neutron at uranium-235.

15) What is nuclear fusion?

16) What does a moderator do to neutrons in a nuclear reactor?

17) Give three sources of background radiation.

18) Give a definition of half-life.

19)* The activity of a radioisotope sample is 840 Bq. Four hours later it has fallen to 105 Bq. Find the half-life of the sample.

20) Which types of radioactive sources are used for the following:
a) smoke detectors, b) sterilisation of food, c) tracers in medicine, d) treating cancer.

21) Explain what kind of damage ionising radiation causes to body cells.

22) List four safety precautions that should be taken when handling radioactive materials in the school lab.

23) What is the main problem with using nuclear power?

24) Give two advantages of using nuclear power to generate electricity.

Index

A

acceleration 84, 85, 89
action forces 88
active transport 28
activity (radioactivity) 100
actual yield 74
aerobic respiration 23
air bags 92
air resistance 87
alkali metals 62
alpha radiation 96, 97,
    102, 103
ammeters 81
anaerobic respiration 24
animal cells 10
anions 49
anomalous results 6, 7
arteries 37
asexual reproduction 18
atomic number 45, 47,
    96
atoms 43-45, 49, 50,
    55, 76
attraction (of charges) 76

B

background radiation 100,
    101
bacterial cells 10
balanced forces 86, 88,
    89
balancing equations 48
bar charts 6
barium meal 53
barium sulfate 53
batteries 79
becquerels (Bq) 100
beta radiation 96, 97,
    102, 103
blood 36
blood vessels 37
braking distances 91
breathing rate 24
bubble wrap 92

C

calculating half-life 101
calculations
    of empirical formulas 73
    of percentage
        composition 72
    of percentage yield 74
    of relative formula mass
        71

cancer 103
capillaries 37
carbohydrases 38
carbon dioxide (test for) 54
carbonates 54
cardiac output (equation) 24
car safety 92
catalysts 67, 70
catalytic converters 70
cations 49
cells (biology) 10
cells (physics) 79
chain reactions 98
charges 76-79
chemical bonds 49
chloride ions (test for) 54
chlorophyll 25
chromatography 59
chromosomes 18, 19
circulatory system 35-37
cloning mammals 20
cold fusion 98
combustion 65
compounds 49-51, 55, 57
concentration (effect on rate
    of reaction) 67, 69
conclusions 8
conservation of momentum 92
controlled assessment 9
correlations 7
covalent bonding 55
covalent substances 56, 57
Crick, Francis 12
crumple zones 92
current 79-83

D

data 6, 7
decay (nuclear) 96, 100
diamond 56
differentiation 21
diffusion 23
digestive system 38-40
diodes 82
direct current (d.c.) 79
displacement 84
displacement reactions 63, 66
distance-time (D-T) graphs 85
distribution (of organisms)
    29-31
DNA 11, 12

E

economic factors 3
eggs 92
electrical power 83
electrons 43, 44 , 49, 50,
    55, 76, 79
electron shells 44, 47, 49,
    50, 55
elements 45-47
empirical formulas 73
endothermic reactions 65
energy 93, 94
energy levels 44
energy transfer in reactions 65
environmental factors 3
enzymes 14-16, 38-40
ethical issues 3
evaluations 8
evidence 1
evolution 33
excess post-exercise oxygen
        consumption (EPOC)
        24
exercise 24
exothermic reactions 65

F

fair tests 2, 5
filament lamps 82
fission 98, 99, 104
fixed resistors 82
flame tests 53
force diagrams 86
forces 86, 88, 89, 92
formulas 51
fossils 33
fractional distillation 58
Franklin, Rosalind 12
friction 76
fuel rods 99
fuel tankers 78
functional foods 41
fusion 98

G

gametes 19
gamma radiation 96, 97,
    102, 103
genes 13
genetic engineering 17
giant molecular substances
        56, 57

Golden Rice 17
grannies 92
graphite 56
gravitational field
        strength (g) 87
gravitational potential
        energy (G.P.E.) 94,
        95
Group 0 elements 64
Group 1 elements 62
Group 7 elements 63
groups in the periodic table
        47, 49, 57, 61-64
growth 34

H

half-life 100, 101
halogens 63
hazards 5
heart 35
heart rate 24
hydrogen halides 63
hypotheses 1

I

immiscible liquids 58
insecticide sprayers 78
insoluble salts 52
insulating materials 76
ionic bonding 49, 50
ionic compounds 50, 51,
        57
ionisation 96
ionising radiation 96, 103
ions 49-51
    tests for 54
isotopes 96

K

kinetic energy (K.E.) 94,
        95

L

laboratory experiments 2
leaves (adaptations for
        photosynthesis) 25
light-dependent resistors
        (LDRs) 82
lightning 77
limewater 54

Index

limiting factors (for photosynthesis) 25
line graphs 7
line of best fit 7
lipase 38
liquids (separation of) 58

M

magnification calculations 11
marble chips 68
mass 87, 89
mass calculations 71, 72
mass number 45, 96
mean (average) 6
meiosis 19
Mendeleev 46
metal halides 63
metallic bonds 61
metals 47, 61
microscopes 11
miscible liquids 58
mitosis 18
moderator 99
momentum 92
motion 88
mutations 13

N

naming compounds 51
negative ions (tests for) 54
neutrons 43, 45, 76, 99
newtons (N) 87
noble gases 64
non-metals 47
nuclear fission 98, 99, 104
nuclear fusion 98
nuclear power 104
nuclear waste 104
nucleus 43, 76

O

ohms 80
old wives' tales 2
organs 35
osmosis 27
oxygen debt 24

P

paint sprayers 78
parallel circuits 80
percentage composition of a compound 72
percentage yield 74
percentile charts 34
periodic table 46, 47
periods (in the periodic table) 47
peristalsis 38
phloem 28
photosynthesis 25, 26
pitfall traps 29
plant cells 10
plant stanol esters 41
plasma 36
platelets 36
pond nets 30
pooters 29
potassium 62
potato murderers 27
potential difference (voltage) 80, 82
potential energy 94, 95
power 83
prebiotics 41
precipitate 54
precipitation reactions 52
predictions 1
principle of the conservation of energy 95
probiotics 41
proteases 38
proteins 13
protons 43-45, 76

Q

quadrats 30, 31

R

radiation sickness 103
radioactive decay 96, 100
radioactive waste 104
radioactivity 96, 97, 100, 102, 103
radon gas 100
range of data 5
rates of reaction 67-70

reaction forces 86, 88
red blood cells 36
relative atomic mass 45, 71
relative formula mass 71
relative mass 43
reliability 2, 5
repelling (of charges) 76
resistance 80-82
respiration 23, 24
resultant forces 88, 89
R_f values 59
risk assessments 5
risks 3, 5
root hair cells 28

S

salts 52
sample size 2
scientists 1
seat belts 92
separating funnels 58
shocks 77, 78
simple molecular substances 56, 57
social factors 3
sparks 77, 78
spectroscopy 54
speed 84, 85
state symbols 48
static electricity 76-78
stem cells 21
sterilisation 102
stomata 25
stopping distances 91
sulfate ions (test for) 52, 54
sweep nets 30

T

tables 6
temperature (effect on rate of reaction) 69
terminal velocity 87
theoretical yield 74
theories 1
thermistors 82
thinking distances 91
tissues 35
tracers 102
transpiration 28

U

unbalanced forces 86, 89

V

vacuum 87
validity 2, 5
variable resistors 81
variables 5
vector quantities 84, 92
veins 37
velocity 84, 85, 87
velocity-time (VT) graphs 85
visking tubing 40
vitrification 104
voltage (potential difference) 80-82
voltmeters 81

W

waste in reactions 74
Watson, James 12
watt 93
weight 87
white blood cells 36
Wilkins, Maurice 12
work done 93

X

X-rays 53
xylem 28

Y

yield 74

Z

zygotes 19

Answers

Revision Summary for B2 Topic 1 (page 22)

4) x 25 magnification

13) pH 1.5

Revision Summary for B2 Topic 2 (page 32)

5) a) 60 beats per minute
   b) 70 beats per minute

16) 5 x 200 = 1000 gnomes

Revision Summary for C2a Topics 1, 2 & 3 (page 60)

10) $CaCO_3 + 2HCl \rightarrow CaCl_2 + H_2O + CO_2$

15) a) KCl b) CaF_2

24) ionic

28)
$$R_f = \frac{\text{distance travelled by substance}}{\text{distance travelled by solvent}}$$

$$= 4.5 \div 12 = 0.375$$

Bottom of page 71

NaOH = 23 + 16 + 1 = 40

Fe_2O_3 = (2 × 56) + (3 × 16) = 160

$MgSO_4$ = 24 + 32 + (16 × 4) = 120

Bottom of page 72

A_r of Ca = 40, A_r of Br = 80,
M_r of $CaBr_2$ = 40 + (2 × 80) = 200

Percentage mass of bromine =
([2 × 80] / 200) × 100 = 80%

Bottom of page 73

	N	H
Mass	84	18
Mass / A_r	84 / 14	18 / 1
	= 6	= 18
Divide by 6	1	: 3

So the empirical formula is NH_3

Revision Summary for C2b Topics 4, 5 & 6 (page 75)

17) a) CO_2 = 12 + (16 × 2) = 44
    b) $MgCO_3$ = 24 + 12 + (16 × 3) = 84
    c) ZnO = 65 + 16 = 81

18) Percentage mass of nitrogen
= ([A_r × n] ÷ M_r) × 100
= ([14 × 1] / 85) × 100 = 16.5%

19)

	Ca	F
Mass	240	228
Mass / A_r	240 / 40	228 / 19
	= 6	= 12
Divide by 6	1	: 2

So the empirical formula is CaF_2

Revision Summary for P2a Topics 1, 2 & 3 (page 90)

13) P = I × V
P = 4.8 A × 230 V = 1104 W

15) s = d ÷ t
s = 3.5 m ÷ 35 s = 0.1 m/s

17) a = (v – u) ÷ t
a = (14 – 0) ÷ 0.4 = 35 m/s²

24) F = m × a
F = 2 kg × 5 m/s² = 10 N

Revision Summary for P2b Topics 4, 5 & 6 (page 105)

3) momentum = mass × velocity
momentum = 78 kg × 15 m/s = 1170 kg m/s

5) E = F × d
E = 535 N × 12 m = 6420 J

7) K.E. = ½ × m × v²
= ½ × 78 kg × (23 m/s)² = 20 631 J

8) G.P.E. = m × g × h (g = 10 N/kg)
= 12 kg × 10 N/kg × 4.5 m
= 540 J

9) K.E. gained = G.P.E. lost (ignoring air resistance).
K.E. = m × g × h
= 78 kg × 10 N/kg × 20 m
= 15 600 J (=15.6 kJ)

19) initial count = 840
after 1 half-life = 840 ÷ 2 = 420
after 2 half-lives = 420 ÷ 2 = 210
after 3 half-lives = 210 ÷ 2 = 105
so, 4 hours must be 3 half-lives.
1 half-life must be 4 ÷ 3 = 1.33 hours